Looking For Muriel

Looking For Muriel:

A Journey Through and Around the Alain Resnais Film

by Darren Arnold

BearManor Media
2022

Looking for Muriel:
A Journey Through and Around the Alain Resnais Film

© 2022 Darren Arnold

All rights reserved.

No portion of this publication may be reproduced, stored, and/or copied electronically (except for academic use as a source), nor transmitted in any form or by any means without the prior written permission of the publisher and/or author.

Published in the United States of America by:

BearManor Media
1317 Edgewater Dr #110
Orlando FL 32804

bearmanormedia.com

Printed in the United States.

Typesetting and layout by John Teehan

ISBN—978-1-62933-860-6

As I was listening to a lot of Woods of Ypres while working on this project, this book is dedicated to the memory of David Gold (1980–2011).

Memory is the diary that we all carry about with us.
— Oscar Wilde,
The Importance of Being Earnest

Contents

Acknowledgements ix

Conventions xi

Introduction 1

Synopsis 9

Chapter 1. Out of Step: *Muriel* in the
    Context of Early 1960s French Cinema 11

Chapter 2. Wartime Burdens: Boulogne
    as a Character in *Muriel* 25

Chapter 3. The Question: *Muriel* and
    Torture in the Algerian War 45

Chapter 4. The Star: Delphine Seyrig
    in *Muriel* 69

Chapter 5. Jackal, Soldier, Antique Dealer:
    Muriel, Malraux, and the OAS 79

Chapter 6. Many Unhappy Returns: *Je t'aime,
    je t'aime* and *Muriel* 99

Chapter 7. Legacy: *Muriel* and Alain Resnais' Post-1960s Output 117

Bibliography 145

Appendix A: Interview with New Wave Editor Ken Rowles 153

Appendix B: Alain Resnais Filmography 163

Appendix C: Photo Credits 167

Acknowledgements

THANKS TO Ben Ohmart, Steve Hills, Ken Rowles, Esther Gold, Stone Wallace, and to my wife and son for tolerating my laptop's near-constant presence on our kitchen table.

Conventions

IN GENERAL, the English-language title is used for any film whose original title is in another language; exceptions to this rule occur where such a film is known internationally by its original title, such as in the case of *Hiroshima mon amour*.

Upon a film's first mention, the original title (if appropriate) and year of release are given in parentheses. Example: *Breathless* (*À bout de souffle*, 1960).

Where a film has an alternative English title, this is given immediately after the first mention of a film, with the titles separated with a forward slash. Example: *Once Upon a Time/Donkey Skin* (*Peau d'âne*, 1970).

For all works cited, the author, year and, where appropriate, page number(s) are given in parentheses for in-text citations, and the full references are listed alphabetically in the bibliography at the end of the book. [Brackets] indicate insertions within quotations.

Unless an English-language source is credited, all translations from French are my own.

Introduction

GIVEN THE SUBJECT of this book—*Muriel, or The Time of Return* (*Muriel, ou le temps d'un retour*, 1963)—and its major theme of memory, it seems quite fitting that I can't remember which I experienced first: the film, or its setting? *Muriel* takes place (and was mostly filmed) in Boulogne-sur-Mer, a French seaport I've become quite familiar with over the past two decades or so, but in terms of when I first encountered Alain Resnais' masterpiece, I honestly cannot establish the correct order of events with any real certainty. It is quite possible that I visited Boulogne as a child—images of a July day featuring bleached-out postcards, seaside souvenirs and a sun-drenched harbor are seared into my psyche—in which case the place most definitely came first for me, but it's also entirely feasible that I'm thinking of a childhood visit to somewhere else in France... or was it Belgium? Such are the vagaries of remembrance. Of course, it may be that these memories have simply been implanted, as in *Blade Runner* (1982), and aren't mine at all—if that's the case, I quietly await the day they come to "retire" me.

This conflation of chronologies would be of more concern to me if it applied to any film other than *Muriel* but, in general, other movies and places give me no such trouble; for example, I know I saw *Welcome to the Sticks* (*Bienvenue chez les Ch'tis*, 2008) and *Disco* (2008)—both in Boulogne, as it happens—before I ever explored their respective settings of Bergues and Le Havre. Similarly, and sticking with movies which were shot not too far from where Alain Resnais filmed *Muriel*, I have no doubt that I first visited Wissant long before *Slack Bay* (*Ma Loute*, 2016) had even been thought of. Perhaps the reason I can easily separate these events is that I first saw each of *Welcome to the Sticks*,

Disco and *Slack Bay* in a cinema; a theatrical screening almost always cements itself in the mind in a way which makes it distinct from the seemingly endless conveyor belt of home viewing. While I am the proud owner of a poster for *Muriel*'s theatrical re-release, I came to the movie via the small screen, which I think is partly why I consider the film and its setting to have no meaningful line of demarcation; the two elements have fused together, forming something of a Möbius strip in my mind. The eerie power of *Muriel* is one which makes it virtually impossible for the viewer to disassociate the film from its setting—and vice versa. Outside and inside of Alain Resnais' film, Boulogne bears some very real, visible scars, and *Muriel* bottles the essence of what one of its main characters dubs "a martyr city".

Unlike Resnais' previous film—*Last Year at Marienbad* (*L'Année dernière à Marienbad*, 1961), which largely thrived on artifice—*Muriel* is very much rooted in reality. The impressive, icy and haunting *Marienbad*, which, inter alia, invites the viewer to ascertain if two people had met previously, takes place entirely within the confines of a luxury hotel and its extensive grounds; as this ornately contrived film's elaborate parlor games unfold, there's a pervasive feeling that, even if the outside world does exist, it may as well not. The Chinese puzzle of *Last Year at Marienbad* plays out in a hermetically sealed test chamber, one populated with unreliable narrators and an oppressive sense of dread. Looking back on the movie in the context of Resnais' oeuvre, you can almost hear the director think to himself: *How might these neuroses manifest themselves in the wider world, should they mingle with everyday problems?* Therefore, the story of *Muriel*, with its recognizably real milieu and troubled characters who circle the plughole as they relive their faltering memories, could be considered to take place in a world where the ghosts of *Marienbad* have been unleashed.

Both *Muriel* and *Last Year at Marienbad* are films which could be said to end rather than conclude; the labyrinth of *Marienbad* eventually leads to a cul-de-sac which provides no real clue as to whether the principal characters had actually met previously, while *Muriel*—despite building to what appears to be a fairly traditional climax—leaves the fate of its main characters unknown as they scatter in various directions during the film's closing moments. Little if anything is resolved in either film, and both *Marienbad* and *Muriel* are as likely to perplex as they are to delight;

it is not difficult to see why those who favor a more orthodox narrative cinema will find these two movies to be willfully obscure. While *Last Year at Marienbad*, given its emphasis on symmetry and mathematical games, may ultimately disappoint those lured into expecting a neat and tidy closure, *Muriel* makes no such promises: for all its intricacies, it's a slice of life, and living is a perpetually messy business, one which tends not to be wrapped up with a bow. *Muriel*, like its predecessor, is immaculately assembled but, paradoxically, it reminds us how untidy and unsatisfactory daily life can be. *Muriel* (and *Marienbad*, for that matter) steadfastly refuses to give up its secrets—no matter how many times you view the film. Some movies tell you everything you need to know after a solitary screening, while others permit you to gradually peel back the layers as you invest in repeat viewings. *Muriel*, however, belongs to an altogether different category: the film that remains something of an enigma irrespective of how—or indeed how often—one approaches it; as such, *Muriel* is as immutable as the towering apartment block in which much of the film's drama unfolds.

Although I may be in some doubt as to which preceded the other, I do know that Boulogne brings me back to *Muriel*, and *Muriel* brings me back to Boulogne. While I don't live too far from Boulogne-sur-Mer, my fascination with *Muriel* cannot simply be attributed to the proximity of its filming location—although this was admittedly quite convenient when it came to undertaking the research for this book. Over the years, the film has risen steadily to the upper echelons of my list of favorite movies, where it continually jostles for position with Jean Eustache's *The Mother and the Whore* (*La maman et la putain*, 1973) and Maurice Pialat's *Under the Sun of Satan* (*Sous le soleil de Satan*, 1987). Many of us recognize that our *favorite* films are not necessarily among the *best* films; for example, I regard *Lawrence of Arabia* (1962) as arguably the greatest film ever made, and I hold tremendous admiration for its incredible technical accomplishments—yet David Lean's epic does not figure among my best-loved movies. Conversely, I can remain fairly objective when assessing the likes of *A Lizard in a Woman's Skin* (*Una lucertola con la pelle di donna*, 1971) and *Mesa of Lost Women* (1953), which I know certainly aren't among the very best films ever made—but both are longstanding favorites of mine; likewise, I have seen far better television than *Bewitched* (1964–1972), yet it remains my TV show of

Muriel's Alphonse (Jean-Pierre Kérien) and Hélène (Delphine Seyrig).

choice. *Muriel*, however, is a film I look on as both a favorite *and* one of the greatest films of the last century; it isn't entirely unique in this regard, given that I consider both *Under the Sun of Satan* and Stanley Kubrick's *Barry Lyndon* (1975) to hold the same status.

So far, *Muriel* has never lost its appeal for me—although that may not be the case once I've completed a book-length study on it. I can think of no other film which nags and gnaws away at me in quite the same way; for days after a viewing of *Muriel*, I find myself troubled and needled by what the film both presents and implies. Few others appear to share my discomfort regarding *Muriel*, so it was a relief to find the author Claude Ollier describing how his "main feeling watching it was pretty soon a rising anxiety, panic even" (Hillier, 1986: 69). Every time I press the button on the player to eject one of my numerous editions of the film, I'm well aware that a case of the howling fantods will follow in very short order. I can think of only two other films which have haunted me in a similar manner: Peter Weir's *Picnic at Hanging Rock* (1975) and Michelangelo Antonioni's *L'Avventura* (1960), both of which, coincidentally or not, end with their riddles unsolved. Robert Benayoun likened *Muriel* to another Antonioni film, *The Eclipse* (*L'Eclisse*, 1962), considering the two, along with Resnais' own *Hiroshima mon amour* (1959) and Louis Malle's *A Very Private Affair* (*Vie privée*, 1962), to be rare examples of cinema which tapped into "a general crisis of desire" (2002: 130).

Yet over the course of repeat viewings, the sense of mystery created by both *Picnic at Hanging Rock* and *L'Avventura* has atrophied, which leads me to ponder if *Muriel*'s impact might be similarly lessened with time? I suspect not. It's as if a reset button is pressed whenever I re-view the film, and I find it impossible to become battle-hardened against it. In fact, the opposite may be true: as my research into the film stepped up, so did the potency of the subject matter. A terrible act of violence lies at the dark heart of *Muriel*—even if, mercifully, this awful deed isn't shown onscreen. Although the film is now nearly sixty years old, the description of torture contained within *Muriel* hasn't lost any of its power to disturb, and it quite daringly flags what was a much wider issue; it is by no means inapt to claim that the use of torture—by both sides—had become commonplace as the war in Algeria escalated. Jean-Luc Godard's unexpectedly brutal *Le petit soldat* (1963) presented an altogether franker depiction of the practice, and the film—which was actually made in 1960—was initially banned, eventually seeing the light of day once the war had ended. Despite covering similar ground to *Muriel*, Godard's film is a quite different animal, and we'll come to consider it in a bit more detail in chapter 3.

Just before beginning work on this book I, like Bernard in *Muriel*, returned to Boulogne. Although I feel as if I know the city fairly well, I was struck by just how much the film had informed my mental image of the town. With *Muriel*, Resnais explored a form of psychogeography which, as absorbing as it is, doesn't give the viewer much of a sense of the layout of the actual city. Occasionally, even those in the film seem to lose their bearings: a character finds that a railway station is no longer served by a route that was firmly in place just a fortnight earlier; two people dispute whether one particular building is on the former site of another; someone else, upon inquiring where the center of town is, learns that they're already standing in it. As an example of how *Muriel* has affected my sense of navigation as far as Boulogne is concerned, I decided to retrace the walk from the train station to the

The main entrance to the *Muriel* building, February 2020.

apartment—a journey detailed in the film's early stages—only to find it to be much shorter than I remembered, and far less convoluted than Resnais' elliptical editing might suggest. As my walk came to its end, I recalled a line spoken by one of *Muriel*'s characters as they traveled between the same points: "We often misjudge distances". What had previously sounded like a throwaway piece of small talk was suddenly reframed as a joke, one which was firmly on me given that I'd been wandering around *Muriel*'s Boulogne—as opposed to the actual one. Will the real Boulogne please stand up?

As I arrived at the *Muriel* apartment (although *not* Muriel's apartment, however tempting it may be to refer to it as that), I stopped to look up at the building; much had changed in over fifty years, yet it was still instantly recognizable as the imposing apartment block from the film. For as long as I can—ahem—recall, a curious detail has been present in the form of a prominent panel above the doorway bearing the English word "building". To the left of the property's entrance, a solitary mock-brass plate remained, yet the darker squares on the roughcast betrayed where considerably more signage, clearly visible in the film, was once sited. A quick inquiry revealed that the medical professional listed on the orphaned plaque appeared to be no longer practicing, and I also discovered that the apartment immediately above the entrance was available for rent. Without any real intention of following up on it, I made a quick note of the agent's telephone number

The lonely sign on the wall of the *Muriel* building, February 2020.

and indulged in a brief moment of fantasy, one that involved taking out a short lease on the perfect backdrop for this project. The prospect of writing and, more crucially, *living* among *Muriel*'s ghosts was as unsettling as it was appealing. As I paused there, buffeted by a vicious wind from the English Channel, I quietly wondered how many of the residents were aware of their building's murky past.

Before you embark on the rest of this book, it is worth highlighting a lengthy piece that appeared in the November 1963 issue of *Cahiers du Cinéma* magazine. This article was actually a transcript of a recording of eight of the magazine's finest contributors discussing *Muriel*, and it makes for absorbing, invigorating reading. However, this debate on *Muriel* illustrates just how far and wide the film sends us when we start to analyze it, and the pages and chapters ahead will provide proof of this. Those at *Cahiers* were given license to wander off topic, and they certainly took advantage of this freedom, although they would always eventually return to the film that underpinned the discussion. *Muriel* may not be the only movie to prompt such branching out, but I am hard pushed to think of any other single film that has sent me into so many diverse areas. You don't *have* to read around *Muriel* but, should you choose to, you will be both surprised and rewarded by what turns up.

In *Muriel, or The Time of Return*, main character Hélène claims to "stick to the same people" as far as her shopping habits are concerned, and on reflection I think it's fair to say that my family and I have done the same over the years in which we've been visiting Boulogne. Yet, this eventually becomes impossible due to the gradual closure of the venues we ritually call in on: the welcoming restaurant in the Brutalist shopping center pulls down its shutters one last time; the huge, well-stocked bookstore closes its doors for good; the wonderful bakery-cum-coffee shop is razed to make way for a slicker, shinier operation; the affable owner of the excellent *friterie* passes away, his stall vanishing from the seafront. Next time we visit, Boulogne's longstanding cinema will almost certainly have shut down and been replaced by a brand new multiplex on the city's left bank. Memory and place. Algeria and France. Resnais and *Muriel*. Time has marched on since I first set foot in Boulogne-sur-Mer—whenever that may have been.

Synopsis

NORTHERN FRANCE, 1962. Widow Hélène Aughain runs an antique business from her cluttered apartment in the seaport of Boulogne-sur-Mer; Hélène lives with her stepson, the jobless Bernard, who has recently returned from military service in Algeria. Bernard claims to have a fiancée—who Hélène hasn't met—named Muriel. Although Hélène is in a relationship with local property magnate Roland de Smoke, she is anxiously awaiting a visit from old flame Alphonse Noyard. Alphonse arrives by train from Paris, and Hélène meets him at the station; to Hélène's mild surprise, Alphonse is accompanied by a young woman he introduces as Françoise, his niece. The three walk back to Hélène's apartment, where they have dinner with Bernard. Alphonse claims to have lived and worked in Algiers in the years between World War II and the present, but is evasive when Bernard asks him for some basic details.

Françoise and Bernard decide to go out for the evening, leaving Hélène and Alphonse to talk; Alphonse then makes a romantic advance toward Hélène, which is rejected. Roland arrives, and he and Hélène head out to the local casino where Hélène, not for the first time, incurs substantial gambling losses. With the apartment to himself, an irritated Alphonse takes the opportunity to snoop around, discovering a record of Bernard's time in Algeria in the form of a diary and some photographs. One of the pictures appears to show a young couple, but one of the faces—most likely Bernard's—has been redacted.

While some of Bernard's time is spent with his casual girlfriend Marie-Do, a large portion of his day is spent obsessing about his deployment in Algeria where, it transpires, he participated in the torture and murder of a young Algerian woman named Muriel. Although Bernard feels tremendous guilt, he believes that most of the blame for Muriel's death lies with his friend Robert, who has also recently returned to Boulogne and is now part of a right-wing paramilitary organization.

In his secluded workshop in the old part of the city, Bernard frequently replays film footage of his time in Algeria; he also takes to traveling around Boulogne in a bid to collect fresh "evidence" using his Super 8 camera and reel-to-reel tape recorder. Françoise, who is actually in a relationship with Alphonse, tells Alphonse she plans to leave him when they eventually get back to Paris. Meanwhile, a new face has arrived in Boulogne in the form of Ernest Choisy, who has been making inquiries about Alphonse.

Sunday lunch at Hélène's is interrupted by Ernest, who reveals that Alphonse has never been to Algiers yet does have both a wife (Simone, Ernest's sister) and a failed restaurant waiting for him back in Paris; Ernest debunks the various other grand claims he suspects Alphonse has made during his stay at Hélène's. Ernest has traveled to Boulogne to ensure that Alphonse returns to Paris, and an argument breaks out between the pair; among other matters, the dispute concerns an unposted letter and Alphonse's failure to inform Hélène of a date Ernest had set with her. The disagreement soon descends into a physical fight; Bernard is highly amused by this and instructs Françoise to fetch his tape recorder, while he gleefully begins filming the spectacle. Françoise brings the recording deck but inadvertently presses the play button, and a cacophony of laughter—presumably a recording of Muriel's torture—emits from the machine. A highly distressed Bernard destroys the tape and flees the apartment; shortly after, he hunts down and kills Robert. Following this, Bernard's workshop is destroyed in an explosion.

Soon after Bernard's departure, everyone else exits the apartment: Françoise leaves alone; Ernest begins to escort Alphonse back to Paris, but Alphonse sneaks away from his brother-in-law and boards a bus bound for Belgium; Hélène runs to the train station in the hope that she might sort out some of the trouble, only to discover that the Paris train now leaves from Boulogne's new station. Simone, who has joined her brother's search for Alphonse, arrives at Hélène's deserted apartment.

Out of Step: *Muriel* In the Context of Early 1960s French Cinema

Chapter One

WHEN WE HEAR MENTION of the French cinema of the early 1960s, we reflexively think of the freewheeling, Paris-set black-and-white films pioneered by the likes of Jean-Luc Godard and François Truffaut, both of whom—along with Claude Chabrol, Éric Rohmer and Jacques Rivette—have endured as the most recognizable faces of the French New Wave. On account of their contributions to legendary French film journal *Cahiers du Cinéma*, these five filmmakers collectively became known as "the *Cahiers* group". These New Wave directors largely abandoned established French filmmaking methods in favor of portable equipment, direct sound, available light and existing locations; such an approach may have been primarily due to a lack of finance, but it resulted in both a paradigm shift and an urgent, raw and immediate form of cinema, one which railed against the sort of modern studio productions putatively dismissed by Truffaut as "le cinéma de papa" (Dad's cinema).

Given the type of cinema the New Wave had established, Alain Resnais' *Muriel, or The Time of Return* appears to be firmly out of step with other French films of the era, so much so that it gives the impression of being completely unaware of any film other than itself. Resnais wasn't closely aligned with the *Cahiers* group, but rather belonged to the *Rive Gauche* (Left Bank) contingent of directors (Paris' world-famous river, the Seine, was used to demarcate the two camps), a group which also included experimental filmmaker Chris Marker, power couple Agnès Varda and Jacques Demy, and Resnais' sometime

François Truffaut in Amsterdam, 1965.

editor Henri Colpi. These directors were, and still are, associated with the New Wave, yet their concerns were rather different from those of their contemporaries just across the river: Left Bank directors saw film as just one of several equally valid art forms, a position which stood in stark contrast to that of the movie-obsessed likes of Godard, Truffaut, et al. While *Muriel* may not have been especially surprising to anyone who had closely tracked Resnais' career to that point, it was certainly far removed from most other French films of the time, which included the likes of *Highway Pickup* (*Chair de poule*, 1963), *Be Careful Ladies* (*Méfiez-vous, mesdames!*, 1963), *Judex* (1963), *War of the Buttons* (*La Guerre des boutons*, 1962), *Any Number Can Win* (*Mélodie en sous-sol*, 1963), and Chabrol's *Bluebeard* (*Landru*, 1963).

Out of Step: *Muriel* in the Context of Early 1960s French Cinema | 13

It is worth taking a moment to recap the steps taken by Alain Resnais en route to *Muriel*: after more than a decade of directing short films—including the Oscar-winning *Van Gogh* (1948)—Resnais made his belated feature debut in 1959 with *Hiroshima mon amour*, a daring and critically-lauded work written by acclaimed novelist Marguerite Duras. What is most striking about this film—which concerns a couple raking over the ashes of the past in post-atomic Hiroshima—is that it at no point feels like a debut; there's a fluency and sureness of touch in evidence which stands at odds with the fidgety, excitable nature of the first features from, say, Truffaut and Godard. While both Truffaut's *The 400 Blows* (*Les quatre cent coups*, 1959) and Godard's *Breathless* (*À bout de souffle*, 1960) are widely, correctly considered to be classics, they nevertheless *feel* like first films, complete with all the energy, hunger and rough edges one would expect to find in inaugural efforts; *Hiroshima mon amour*, on the other hand, exhibits the style and confidence of a seasoned, established filmmaker. It also contains:

> what well may be the ghastliest five minutes ever recorded on commercial film. The scene shifts rapidly from a shot of the Hiroshima museum, to some of the relics of the attack, to graphic sections of film taken in Hiroshima immediately after the bombing. Terrified men and women swim, in flame covered rivers; thousands of people, living and dead, huddle in makeshift hospital-shelters. Director Alain Resnais spares the viewer nothing—the camera methodically records all of the most gruesome effects of immediate radiation burn and lingering radiation sickness, and it is often a few moments before the viewer realizes the full horror of what he has just seen. (Quint, 1960)

Resnais followed this stunning debut with what remains his best-known work, *Last Year at Marienbad*, an elegant, baffling memory puzzle from the pen of another renowned writer, Alain Robbe-Grillet. *Marienbad* won the Golden Lion at the 1961 Venice Film Festival, and the movie's cultural impact cannot be overstated:

> In two months, just in Paris, the film exceeds a hundred thousand admissions. A reporter summarizes the climate around this phenomenon: "What! You're telling me you haven't seen *Marienbad*!... and they looked at me as if I had never heard [Beethoven's] Ninth nor read [Stendhal's] *La Chartreuse*". The diners in town talk only of *Marienbad*, and in the Latin Quarter students and teachers are recreating *Marienbad*. [French newspaper] *Le Monde* launches a big investigation: "For or against *Marienbad*?" Three hundred readers respond. During a month and a half, a page a day will be devoted to the film in the newspaper. Probably no other film has generated as many articles and contradictory interpretations. [...] *Marienbad* is not only a topic of discussion of aesthetics, but a phenomenon that affects the wider public. Soon, women start to adopt *Marienbad* hairstyles, and we endlessly play the "*Marienbad* game" [Nim] with matches. (Brangé, 2018: 13–14)

In the timeline of Resnais' career, *Marienbad* brings us up to *Muriel* and its somewhat anomalous position in the cinema of the day. While Resnais had enjoyed real success with his first two feature films, there was always the sense that his work, like that of many others among the New Wave and its associated movements, was far more likely to command the respect of his peers than it was to win over the man in the street. Resnais, like many of his contemporaries, could be considered to be a director's director, and such status might lead one to conclude that his work would, to a degree at least, be immune to criticism when it came under the scrutiny of those filmmakers on either immediate side of the Seine—although any such exemption, naturally, would not be applied by those whose job it was to review the films the public would pay to see. Therefore, when *Muriel* was finally released, it was perhaps not especially surprising that reviewers did not know what to make of it, and François Truffaut, in a chapter titled "My Friends in the New Wave" in his essay collection *The Films in My Life*, outlined the extent of the film's critical opprobrium:

[*Muriel*'s] reception was very severe: the critics were disarmed and unjust at the same time. Resnais is the most professional of French directors and one of those rare filmmakers who is an artist. There are any number of ways of constructing a screenplay, and many ways of filming it. It is evident that Resnais envisages all of them, makes his choice, and carefully manages every detail of the enterprise, unlike so many directors who work haphazardly, building their plots any old way, filming confused ideas confusedly. (1985: 327–328)

Given the highly ambitious nature of *Muriel*, such a reaction was perhaps to be expected. However, it wasn't just the critics who were left bemused (or, as Truffaut put it, "disarmed") by *Muriel*'s unusual filmic grammar: Truffaut, somewhat surprisingly, came across as equivocal when revealing his own response to his friend's film:

I have already seen *Muriel* three times without liking it completely, and maybe not liking the same things each time I saw it. I know that I'll see it again many times. Certainly the critics are right to be demanding with a man of Resnais's importance, a man esteemed and recognized throughout the world—but the shots leveled at *Muriel* were rarely aimed at the heart of the subject, but rather at its extremities. (ibid.: 328)

It is perhaps a little too easy to center on some of the relatively negative entries among the initial responses to *Muriel*, but it is nevertheless interesting to note how Resnais wasn't given a free ride by his peers—there was no noticeable closing of ranks among his fellow directors. That said, the 1960s was a time—at least in France—where critics could become filmmakers yet remain critics, and the appetite of those in the *Cahiers* group (and beyond) for appraising and dissecting film continued long after these directors had made their feature debuts. Considering the creative evolution of the members of this set, Richard Brody noted how "[t]heir criticism didn't just foretell and inspire their movies, but also became integrated into them" (2010). As Truffaut's comments on *Muriel* prove, it was certainly a film which both critics and filmmakers were keen to discuss, no matter their position on this apparently baffling picture. Even if the jury was out on the merits of *Muriel*, the *Marienbad*-like amount of time and space given to its analysis proved that Resnais' film was to be dismissed at one's peril; it's almost as if the film's special qualities had been broadly identified but had yet to be pinpointed. In the above quote from Truffaut, he attests to the film's replay value; whatever that certain something may have been, it kept bringing him back to *Muriel*.

It is also worth noting how, in the very same quote, Truffaut points out that it was Resnais' standing as a purveyor of impeccable cinematic fare that had attracted some lukewarm notices as far as *Muriel* was concerned. The implication of this was that a lesser filmmaker wouldn't have been subjected to the same level of rigorous scrutiny as that afforded to Resnais. Truffaut's remarks appear to both side with the critics and pay something of a backhanded compliment to the director of *Muriel*: after just two feature films, Resnais had set the bar unrealistically high. The passage of time has allowed us to look back on *Muriel* as a sort of synthesis of Alain Resnais' previous two features, one which featured a distillation and refinement of the themes he had begun teasing out in *Hiroshima mon amour* and *Last Year at Marienbad*; as such, *Muriel* is a palimpsest, with the specters of its predecessors lurking around the edges of the screen. The title of Alain Resnais' penultimate film—*You Ain't Seen Nothin' Yet* (*Vous n'avez encore rien vu*, 2012)—serves as a wry warning from the future for those who, having been weaned on *Hiroshima* and *Marienbad* as they work through Resnais' filmography, are about to approach *Muriel*.

There is a chance that *Muriel* simply proved to be a little overwhelming for those who encountered it on its initial release; on first viewing, it appears to be an impossibly dense work which requires much decoding, and audiences of the early 1960s did not have anything like the present-day home entertainment options at their disposal to facilitate repeat viewings. Following its screening at the 1963 New York Film Festival, *The New York Times*' reviewer Eugene Archer concluded that *Muriel* "was impossible to understand after a single viewing" (1963, as cited in Robson, 2017). There can be no doubt that *Muriel* was, and remains, a difficult film, and its daunting, sophisticated demeanor hasn't faded in the slightest since it debuted in cinemas. It is by no means wide of the mark to take the view that "the desire for illumination is just what Resnais is seeking to frustrate. He's imparting a mood, not transmitting a message" (ibid.).

Considering its slightly shaky start, it's quite reasonable to say that *Muriel* stood a fair chance of becoming a *film maudit*: its unorthodox treatment of a difficult subject matter—not to mention the critical reviews—appeared sufficient to relegate the movie to 1963's cinematic footnotes, especially in the face of infinitely more accessible competition. Yet *Muriel* was kept alive partly because people were loath to stop analyzing it, which perhaps proves that there really is no such thing as bad publicity. Whether you liked *Muriel* or not, Alain Resnais had painstakingly created a work which simply *had* to be talked about. In the aforementioned lengthy, wide-ranging discussion published in *Cahiers* under the rather telling title "Les Malheurs de *Muriel*" ("The Misfortunes of *Muriel*"), the film critic Jean Domarchi detailed what he considered to be the film's main shortcoming:

> What cinema needs to reflect is the organic whole—in precisely the way that all the great American films reflected American society and everything that determined it. I have no sense of that in Resnais. If *Muriel* is truly, as has been claimed, a committed film, and if it's at the same time a profoundly personal film, an autobiography, then I'm forced to call it a failure because in terms of committed cinema it does not aim at the organic whole, i.e. the whole of a society viewed through a particular situation; and in terms of Resnais's autobiography, it reveals only a pure particularity which fails to relate to the universal. (Hillier, 1986: 72)

These comments certainly back up the notion that there was "a very clear sense that Resnais [was] perceived as being very different from the *Cahiers* group in the *nouvelle vague* [New Wave] and as being in the vanguard of developments in "modern" cinema in a way that the *Cahiers* group was not" (ibid.: 29). *Muriel* is a pitiless film, and in this sense it has much more in common with certain French movies from the first half of the 1970s—including Jean Eustache's *The Mother and the Whore*, Maurice Pialat's *The Mouth Agape* (*La gueule ouverte*, 1974) and Claude Chabrol's *Pleasure Party/A Piece of Pleasure* (*Une partie de plaisir*, 1975)—than it does with anything the *Cahiers* group served up in the decade of *Muriel*'s release. However, it should be mentioned that the above-quoted discussion also involved Jacques Rivette, whose reaction to *Muriel* was generally favorable. Moreover, the magazine, in a March 1965 article titled "Twenty Years of French Cinema: The Best French Films since the Liberation" included both *Muriel, or The Time of Return* and *Hiroshima mon amour* in its top 10, where they rubbed shoulders with works from luminaries such as Jean Renoir, Robert Bresson (whose *Pickpocket* [1959] nabbed the top spot), and Jean Cocteau (ibid.: 82). While there was no place for *Last Year at Marienbad*, a third Resnais film—the short documentary *Night and Fog* (*Nuit et brouillard*, 1956)—featured in the list, where it just grazed the top forty. Apparently, it had taken just a couple of short years for *Cahiers* to iron out their initial misgivings regarding *Muriel* and/or its director.

Whereas many New Wave films tended to point to the future (or at least the present) as they sought to break new ground, *Muriel* is a somber, downbeat work which looks conspicuously to the past. This isn't to say that *Muriel* isn't a pioneering work, but it's one that marches to its own tune, and the film cannot be viewed as part of the wider movement that was taking place in France at that time. Additionally, given that *Muriel* was set, and mostly filmed, in the northern city of Boulogne-sur-Mer, it presented a very different France from the chic Paris many will associate with the New Wave. *Cahiers* group lynchpin Jean-Luc Godard's glib insistence that all you needed for a movie was a girl and a gun conjured up images of coffee-and-Gitanes-fueled escapades in the French capital, and such events seemed a world away from *Muriel*'s ostensibly provincial concerns—even if Resnais' film actually did include both of the ingredients prescribed by Godard. When questioned on the uneasiness that was so prevalent in *Muriel*'s representation of the quotidian, Resnais replied:

> There is, I believe, in *Muriel*, a critique of the [magazine] *France Dimanche*-style idea of happiness, of the comfortable little happiness based on hangouts and

readymade ideas. Perhaps some spectators will be led by these images to ask themselves: "Is this really what we want?" […] We also wanted to show in *Muriel* that horror, crime, violence are not, naturally, in life, surrounded by climates of horror, crime, violence. We are all capable of dealing with horror without realizing it. We are all able to conduct ourselves in ways that later on appear incomprehensible, inexplicable (which is precisely the problem and the shame of a character in *Muriel*). The characters are not always up to the fates. Often, in the cinema, there is a notion that great events produce great characters. I thought that for once we could maybe show characters smaller than the events they come across and that would, in a way, give awareness to the true dimension of those events. (Bounoure, 1962)

Furthermore, *Muriel* was Resnais' first color feature, and this departure from monochrome doesn't really fit with our collective memory of French cinema of the early 1960s. Yet in technical terms, it's not just *Muriel*'s Eastmancolor film stock that separates it from much of the typical New Wave output of the late 50s and early 60s. Whereas the shooting of many New Wave titles, as outlined earlier, was characterized by rather chaotic methods which bordered on guerrilla filmmaking, *Muriel*—like Resnais' previous two features—was the result of a precise, measured and highly controlled production. Although most of the film was shot in Boulogne, the scenes in the main character's home were actually filmed on a Paris soundstage using an exact replica of a real apartment in Boulogne; this move goes firmly against the New Wave's common practice of filming in existing locations.

The film's editing alone counts as a monumental feat—it's estimated that *Muriel* consists of around one thousand shots, which is more than double the number found in a typical film of equivalent length. Irrespective of any doubts his fellow filmmakers may have had regarding *Muriel* as a whole, its director's expertise in the editing suite—in the mid-1940s, Resnais had trained as a film editor—did not go unrecognized by his peers:

> In 1959 [Jean-Luc] Godard argued that Resnais was "the second greatest editor in the world, after Eisenstein". A viewing of *Le chant du Styrène* (1958) led him to say that Resnais "has invented the modern tracking shot". He ranked *Hiroshima mon amour* among the ten best films of 1959, as he would *Muriel* among the ten best of 1963. Godard, then, valued Resnais very highly. In the 70s, however, he showed himself to be rather more exacting. Nevertheless, it could be argued that the dialogue between the two filmmakers has never ended. In 1974 Godard claimed that there were many ways of making films, notably "like Alain Resnais, who makes sculpture". (Leutrat, 2000: 66)

Godard, ever the curmudgeon, has not always been so forthcoming with praise for his fellow filmmakers, so his comments should not be taken lightly (for more detail on the editing in both *Muriel* and Godard's own work, please see Appendix A). However, not everyone was as enamored with Resnais' skills in the cutting room, with Pauline Kael commenting, "Resnais's editing of *Muriel* [is] so fast that you can't keep track of what's going on" (1965: 21). Certainly, Kael's argument appears to be backed up by the fact that the film's opening scene sees more than twenty-three cuts occur in no more than thirty seconds (Sharpe, 2012). While the fizzing editorial technique on display in *Muriel* is certainly quite breathtaking, closer inspection of it gives the impression that the film was shot as a fairly straightforward realist drama, before being carefully cut into wafer-thin slices and subsequently transmogrified into something of much greater complexity.

Muriel's insistent operatic score (by German composer Hans Werner Henze) serves to further distance the film from realism, and there is the sense that, if this music was removed and *Muriel*'s scenes reshuffled, we would then be presented with a reasonably conventional piece of narrative cinema. As Susan Sontag noted, "It is rather as if Resnais had taken a story, which could be told quite straightforwardly, and cut it against the grain [....] [A]lthough the story is not difficult to follow, Resnais' techniques for telling it deliberately estrange the viewer" (1964). To put this theory to the test, please take a moment to revisit the synopsis which appears immediately before this chapter:

Out of Step: *Muriel* in the Context of Early 1960s French Cinema | 21

The sign for the street where much of *Muriel* unfolds, October 2019.

while *Muriel* is not the easiest of films to summarize, the outline *should* read as the sort of linear narrative Sontag had in mind. As a side note, given Godard's comment above regarding how Resnais had pioneered the tracking shot, it seemed willfully perverse that *Muriel*, but for one significant instance, was almost entirely shot using static camera setups.

Study of Jean Cayrol's screenplay for *Muriel* reveals a meticulous work which maps out the intricate edits visible in the finished film. This proves, perhaps surprisingly, that *Muriel* closely followed its writer's intentions, and the complexity of what's seen on the page is mirrored onscreen; Cayrol, like Resnais, had real knowledge of film editing and was able to incorporate this into his writing. Thus, it could be said that no less than *six* people contributed to making *Muriel* the triumph of montage it so clearly is: Cayrol, Resnais, editors Kenout Peltier and Eric Pluet, and assistant editors Claudine Merlin and Svetla Pingova.

Significantly, *Muriel*'s published screenplay bears the names of both Cayrol and Resnais—although the latter is only credited for his direction—which reveals the symbiotic nature of the project; indeed, Cayrol and Resnais' credits on *Muriel* appear onscreen simultaneously, with the screenwriter's name the marginally more prominent of the two. Resnais, in another move which set him apart from the New Wave and the auteur theory the movement was largely synonymous with, was always credited with the *réalisation* (direction) of his films, rejecting the *un film de* (a film by) label so common in French cinema. Cayrol's script also contains a wealth of detail that isn't apparent in the finished film—through his screenplay we learn, for example, that the story takes place between Saturday, September 29, 1962, and Sunday, October 14, 1962 (1963: 41, 121). In her review of the movie in *Film Quarterly*, Susan Sontag was of the impression that *Muriel*'s story takes place over the course of several months, which says much about Resnais' ability to manipulate time (1964).

The exacting nature of *Muriel*'s creation is borne out by the fact that its shoot, which lasted for around three months, stands as the longest in Resnais' career; this is quite remarkable considering that it was only his third feature, and he continued making films for more than half a century following its release. That Resnais and his cast and crew filmed each scene exactly one week after the dates given in Cayrol's script is testament to the rigorousness of the shoot (Leutrat and Liandrat-Guigues, 2006: 225). Such a rigid framework, of course, meant that Resnais, in a rare nod to the working practices typically employed by New Wave directors, was limited to working with whatever the light and weather conditions were at the time a scene was due to be filmed, with the director recalling how he and the rest of the crew "would not try to change the slightest thing for the colour. If it was raining, there would be rain. If there was sun there would be sun. We wouldn't pay any attention to that" (Monaco, 1979: 90).

Muriel weaves a tangled web, but perhaps it is now time to think on ways in which we might make the film more accessible. Those looking to move toward an understanding of the film will find it somewhat reassuring to discover that Susan Sontag claimed that "*Muriel*, like *L'Année dernière à Marienbad*, should not puzzle, because there is nothing 'behind' the lean, staccato statements that one sees. They can't be deciphered, because they don't say more than they say" (1964). It is important to note that the storytelling in *Muriel*, while often jagged, fragmented and elliptical, is always chronological, a fact which frequently proves quite surprising to those who've just experienced their maiden voyage in *Muriel*'s admittedly choppy waters.

It is not readily apparent, but *Muriel*'s structure is much like that of *Last Year at Marienbad*—only in reverse; if *Marienbad* is a coil being tightly wound, then *Muriel* represents a helix unraveling. André S. Labarthe described how "the film starts out apparently as a straight line which then pulls you into a kind of circular movement", while, in the same discussion, Jacques Rivette noted how *Muriel* "has an extremely logical and mathematical construction, just like a thriller. But it doesn't tell you about one investigation, there are two or three or more, all overlapping" (Hillier, 1986: 70). The cardioid nature of *Muriel* could be said to extend way beyond the frame, given the myriad subjects that surround the film. *Muriel* appears complicated, but look closely and you'll see that it is possible to make order from its extreme Venn diagram.

Given that a fair portion of this section of the book has looked at how *Muriel* diverged from much of the surrounding New Wave output, it seems fitting to close out this chapter with the words of François Truffaut who, despite harboring some initial reservations as outlined earlier, was among the first to streamline *Muriel* with this most perceptive observation: "In *Muriel*, Resnais treats the same subject that Renoir treated in *La Règle du Jeu* [The Rules of the Game, 1939] and Chabrol in *Les Bonnes Femmes* [Good Time Girls, 1960]: we act out *Punch and Judy* as we wait to die" (1985: 328).

An aerial view of Boulogne-sur-Mer.

Wartime Burdens: Boulogne As a Character In *Muriel*

Chapter Two

DURING THE NAPOLEONIC WARS, the eponymous emperor gathered his famed *Grande Armée* (Great Army) in Boulogne-sur-Mer, and this act is commemorated by an impressive Corinthian order column which stands on a hill between Boulogne and neighboring Wimereux. The city has several other claims to fame, including the Declaration of Boulogne, a 1905 document which cemented the foundations for constructed language Esperanto. Boulogne has also been at the vanguard of medical progress: in 1800, some of the very first smallpox vaccinations were administered in the city and, just a few years later, Napoleon demanded his soldiers be inoculated against the disease (Empson, 1996). From these limited examples, it's clear to see that Boulogne has been at the center of some important historical developments, so it is unfortunate that the city is nowadays chiefly associated with the bombardment of World War II (WWII).

It's reasonable to assume that, as far as Boulogne is concerned, the Second World War is at the forefront of people's thinking due to it being a more recent event than the mobilizing (and vaccinating) of Bonaparte's troops or the ratification of L. L. Zamenhof's auxiliary language. Yet there are notable facts concerning present-day Boulogne which still can't throw off the shadow of the war—for example, for the past thirty years, Boulogne has been the home of France's expansive National Sea Center, which stands as the largest public aquarium in the entire continent. Staying with the aquatic theme, the city enjoys the status of Europe's largest seafood processing center, and every year

A catch of tuna fish being unloaded in Boulogne.

sees around 350,000 metric tons of fish handled in Boulogne; I'd like to think there's no link between this activity and the aquarium. Yet these prominent statistics are eclipsed by the devastation Boulogne endured during WWII, which retains a queasy power to overshadow events before or since.

Boulogne, like much of northern France, was in the thick of it during World War I (WWI), when the city served as one of the chief hospital areas, yet it wasn't until WWII that Boulogne witnessed the wholesale destruction which has since imprinted on its collective consciousness. The conflict was in its incipient stages when the city came under attack from the Wehrmacht:

> [A]s Allied troops were retreating from Belgium and northern France, German panzer and motorized infantry columns were beginning to encircle Boulogne and Calais on 23 May [1940]. One million Allied troops, including the bulk of the BEF [British Expeditionary Force], were trapped in a tightening noose. On the same day, having

retreated from Belgium, [French officer Daniel] Barlone and his unit found themselves in deep countryside south of Lille with little access to news. But he managed to learn that [French general Maurice] Gamelin had been replaced by [Maxime] Weygand ("he will surely pull us through"), and then the rumour was confirmed that the Germans had reached Boulogne. (Carswell, 2019: 75–76)

By the date given in the above quote, the Battle of Boulogne—which constituted part of the Battle of France—was in the second of its four days. General Gamelin, whose command of the French Army during the Battle of France was nothing short of disastrous, mistakenly believed that the Germans' chief objective was Paris. Having arranged his troops accordingly, the French coast was left underdefended. The Battle of Boulogne commenced the day after outnumbered French and British troops had sprung a morale-boosting (and Hitler-rattling) counterattack in their defeat by Rommel's forces at Arras, a beautiful city which lies roughly seventy miles inland of Boulogne and bears the dubious honor of having a battle named for it in both world wars. During the Battle of Boulogne, French, British and Belgian troops attempted to repel the German attack but were eventually overrun, and the city was captured.

Simultaneously, and just a few miles up the coast, the same belligerents were involved as the Siege of Calais played out to the same result. Shortly after, and to the great shock of the world, France fell and its Third Republic collapsed. While Calais and Boulogne were captured swiftly, far worse was to come as the two cities endured four years of intense, fiery warfare that melted each port to its core. Some years ago, I was in Calais at the end of a long, hot summer during which, I can only presume, tensions between carnies and locals had been running high; while sitting in the old town's main square, I witnessed a particularly ferocious Hey Rube play out in the area immediately next to the city's thirteenth-century watchtower. The Calais police soon got a grip on the situation, but not before a fair amount of blood was spilled, the sight of which immediately made me think of what the town suffered during WWII. Of course, this relatively minor fracas was nothing compared to the death and destruction that would occur on a frequent basis in the Calais of the 1940s, but the unpleasant spectacle nevertheless highlighted how, for so many of us, the carnage of the Second World War is of a scale that we can never properly comprehend.

Boulogne's harbor and vicinity were completely destroyed in the wake of D-Day, with Tallboys—12,000-pound seismic bombs—inflicting much of the damage. This prompted the Axis powers to reevaluate their options, and in August 1944 Hitler made Boulogne one of the Atlantic Wall's strongholds. However, just one month later, Boulogne was liberated following the successful execution of Operation Wellhit, which saw Canadian troops take the city after a six-day assault. Perhaps it is small wonder, then, that Boulogne-sur-Mer has become synonymous with what it experienced during the war.

In Boulogne's old town, not far from a statue of smallpox vaccine pioneer Edward Jenner, stands the city's war memorial. Northern France is home to countless such monuments, and a visit to any one allows for some sober reflection on the horrors inflicted on this part of the world. The cumulative chilling effect of the names carved on Boulogne's memorial, however, places it in an altogether different

Calais, May 1940.

sphere. Situated in the city's Boulevard Eurvin, this huge marble structure, which has a surface area of over 7500 square feet and stands 20 feet high, crystallizes Boulogne's terrible losses from multiple conflicts. During WWI, fifty civilian deaths occurred in Boulogne, a fairly low figure compared to the 1600-plus Boulogne natives who died in combat during the same conflict. In addition to the names of the residents who perished in the two world wars (in both cases, there are separate lists for military and civilians), the monument also marks those who were deported from the city during the German occupation of World War II, as well as the local members of the French Resistance who died during the same conflict. Furthermore, there are sections for the Boulogne natives who died in Indochina and the dozen local military deaths which occurred in North Africa—of course, the latter category has particular relevance to *Muriel*. It is most likely no coincidence that *Muriel*'s workroom, where the troubled Bernard pays his own idiosyncratic tribute to one particular casualty of war, is close to Boulogne's memorial.

Boulogne's war memorial.

As is to be expected, the catalog of names on the war memorial makes for dispiriting, upsetting reading, but it is an inversion of statistics that is particularly troubling: in stark contrast to the city's numbers for the Great War, WWII saw Boulogne's civilian deaths exceed its military casualties. Early on in *Muriel*, main character Hélène, when asked about Boulogne's WWII legacy, replies, "Many died, many were shot… I can't remember how many… two hundred, three thousand… I can't really remember". Given that there are around six hundred civilian dead listed in the WWII section on Boulogne's war memorial, neither of Hélène's estimates comes remotely close to the real figure. It is not hard to see why *Muriel*'s director didn't like these characters (Monaco, 1979: 87). Through both *Night and Fog* and *Hiroshima mon amour*, Alain Resnais had already examined some of WWII's worst atrocities and consequently would have had little time for someone— fictitious as they were—who didn't know the most basic of wartime facts about their hometown. Certainly, Boulogne's war dead deserve more respect than that afforded by Hélène's nonchalant guesswork; while relaying these numbers, her distracted tone is similar to that of someone attempting, without much success, to recall a shopping list.

Yet it is perhaps a little too easy to blame Hélène for such vagaries of memory, and we should not forget that she survived the war in a part of France which, by the early 1940s, had begun to resemble hell on earth. Hélène recalls some of the details of the morning after an air raid: "ashes on my fingers… rain fell onto Bernard's little bed… he was still terrified… the silverware had melted on the floor"; toward the end of the film, Bernard speaks of the snow that fell on his bed during the same incident, and this marks what is the film's starkest depiction of how recollections of the same event can vary from person to person (Hélène still insists it was rain). Yet it is fairly clear that not all of Hélène's demons can be attributed to what she experienced during the Second World War:

> Appearing at points anxious, nostalgic, unpredictable, capricious, depressed, forgetful, erratic and neurotic, Hélène's behaviour in the film certainly bears witness to the presence of an underlying psychic disturbance, although the origins (physical or mental) and/or perpetrators(s)

of this disturbance are at no point made explicit. Yet it is perhaps precisely this absence of origin that is most revealing about Hélène's symptoms, which certain theorists have loosely associated with the trauma victim [...]. [...] Hélène's behaviour subscribes to a comparatively contemporary conception of trauma, that is, the possession of a repressed memory relived repeatedly in the present through nightmarish visions and fragmented episodes. (Sharpe, 2012)

It is quite apparent that Hélène, as with the unnamed character Delphine Seyrig played in *Last Year at Marienbad*, is constantly on the run from something in her psyche (unlike Alphonse, who starts and ends the film quite literally on the run from the various problems he's authored), and her breezy, fidgety and frequently sunny demeanor belies a soul in torment. Whether the root cause of Hélène's damage is something as relatively benign as unrequited love is never made clear, but there's one subtle, fleeting glimpse as to what her monster in the closet may be when a snoozing Alphonse grabs her wrist. While most viewers will peg Alphonse for a snake as soon as he enters the film, this ugly rearing of his potentially abusive tendencies casts him in a whole new light. Conversely, the notion that he may have been violent toward Hélène during their relationship is one that engenders viewer sympathy for the jittery antique dealer. With this development in mind, we really *should* forgive her error regarding Boulogne's wartime death toll. Whether it's the war, domestic violence, some other trauma, or a combination of these that weighs so heavily on Hélène, she appears to employ a coping strategy in the form of her nocturnal visits to the casino. To paraphrase Stephen King: if Hélène's mind is a blackboard, gambling is the eraser (2013). Hélène also looks to the quotidian to distract her, and while there's something to be said for using the everyday to counter a period of upheaval, in Hélène's case the background noise is simply too loud to be drowned out by the mundane:

> Maybe dullness is associated with psychic pain, because something that's dull or opaque fails to provide enough stimulation to distract people from some other, deeper

type of pain that is always there, if only in an ambient low-level way, and which most of us spend nearly all our time and energy trying to distract ourselves from. (Wallace, 2011)

While the insufficiency of memory (such as Hélène's) was arguably the key theme in *Hiroshima mon amour*, a story that also played out against the backdrop of a city bearing the heavy scars of war, *Muriel* sees Resnais divide his attention more evenly as he places roughly equal emphasis on memory and place. While it wouldn't be wholly accurate to view *Hiroshima mon amour* as a dry run for *Muriel*, the latter proves that Resnais had virtually perfected the themes he had begun developing in his debut feature. Of course, in between these two films, Resnais had directed *Last Year at Marienbad*, a film which allowed him to forensically examine the concept of memory in an environment free of the historical burdens shared by Hiroshima and Boulogne. In *Last Year at Marienbad*, the spa town of the title may or may not be where the film's two central characters met the year before—if indeed they did meet previously—but a sense of place certainly isn't critical in the way it is for both *Hiroshima mon amour* and, especially, *Muriel*. It is quite revealing that *Muriel* is the first feature film by Resnais to omit a place name from its title; Boulogne is such a huge part of the film—paradoxically, even more significant than Muriel herself—that to feature the city's name in the title would almost be overkill, and Resnais was nothing if not a subtle filmmaker.

Given that it was the scene of some of the most ferocious fighting in the European theater of WWII, Boulogne was largely, hurriedly rebuilt in the conflict's immediate aftermath. As such, its similarities to the Hiroshima of Resnais' debut feature are obvious. A walk around Boulogne reveals how the city rapidly becomes "older" as one gets further away from the seafront, and in a matter of minutes the functional, hastily-erected postwar buildings soon give way to more ornate structures: a spectacular basilica dating back to the reign of King Louis Philippe I; a bust of Esperanto inventor Zamenhof; the quaint train station featured so prominently in *Muriel*; and, most impressive of all, a thirteenth-century castle and its magnificent ramparts. This dichotomy is mirrored in the interior of Hélène's apartment, where an incongruous assortment of antiques prompts Bernard to quip, "You never know what you'll wake up to in this place… the Second Empire or rustic Normandy". This jumble of antiques led to one critic memorably labelling Hélène's seaside residence as an "apartment for shipwrecks" (Benayoun, 2002: 133).

As with most everything in *Muriel*, it seems that the occupation assigned to Hélène isn't some random, interchangeable one, given how antiques are intertwined with memories—even if such memories often belong to others. Furthermore, the antique trade is one in which fakes—and how to spot them—are all part of the job, even if Hélène seems oddly reluctant to peg the phony Alphonse for what he really is. Robert Benayoun touches on an interesting aspect of *Muriel* in pointing out that "Hélène lives with her false son, just like Alphonse will bring his false niece" (ibid.). While the latter statement certainly seems fair, the former is both quite harsh and far removed from the French term for stepson (*beau-fils*, literally "beautiful son").

Boulogne's architectural duality is easily explained: during the Second World War, the port formed part of the Atlantic Wall and was therefore of premium strategic importance, although General Gamelin had completely failed to foresee this eventuality. Given this status, less emphasis was placed on attacking the town beyond the stretches which lay immediately next to the sea, although the bombs didn't always discriminate. It is a sad fact that many of the civilians killed in Boulogne died as a result of Allied air raids, and the city was by no means the only port to suffer in such a way:

> France's Channel ports […] were among the closest Axis targets to Britain. Le Havre […] endured over 140 raids during the German occupation, or an average of one every ten days; closer ports like Boulogne suffered more. The need to prevent a German invasion of the UK in 1940 involved attacks on the build-up of German shipping and barges in French ports between Calais and Le Havre, as well as on Luftwaffe airfields in France. The most intensive attacks on what became known as "Blackpool front"— the Channel ports on either side of Calais [Dunkirk, Boulogne]—took place on 7 September 1940, when the

> invasion of Britain was seen as imminent. They accounted for most of the 292 French identified as killed in British raids during 1940. (Baldoli and Knapp, 2012: 25–26)

Over the course of the war, Boulogne itself was subjected to more than five hundred air raids, and it was the quite visible traces of the bombardment which led Jean Cayrol to suggest *la nouvelle Boulogne* (new Boulogne) as the setting for *Muriel* (Chick, 2011: 79). While immersed in *Muriel*'s world, it is tempting to think that Boulogne's misfortune was somehow unique, yet the above statistics highlight the sustained nature of the Allies' attacks on these German-occupied ports. With this in mind, it's easy to understand why the director also considered Brest, in his native Brittany, as a backdrop for the tangled story of *Muriel*. Brest, like Boulogne, is a port city that was virtually razed to the ground during World War II, leading to postwar reconstruction on an unprecedented scale:

> Brest [...] became a major Bomber Command target because of the German surface vessels [...] docked there from late 1940. From 4 January 1941 to 12 February 1942, Brest received 25 major raids (of over 50 heavy bombers) and numerous smaller ones—a total of 1,655 tons of bombs. In March and April 1941, indeed, the port attracted over half of Bomber Command's (still modest) effort. The raids did some damage to the German ships and encouraged them to flee. They also, however, killed 207 *Brestois* [inhabitants of Brest; emphasis added], and seriously injured 336, as well as forcing many others away from home at night as bombs destroyed steadily more of their city. (Baldoli and Knapp, 2012: 26)

While it's now impossible to imagine *Muriel* being set anywhere other than Boulogne—*Muriel* and the city have become enmeshed ever since Alain Resnais commenced shooting the film in late 1962—the possibility of the story taking place in Brest illustrates Resnais' key logistical requirement for the film: *Muriel* simply had to occur in a place where the past had been erased and subsequently reconstructed.

The *Muriel* building, February 2020.

There is arguably nowhere in Boulogne as representative of its unwanted makeover as the huge, sprawling Boulevard Gambetta. This area was once composed of beautiful buildings—cafés, restaurants, luxury hotels and so on, which were replaced, postwar, by four imposing, brutalist buildings, each of which consists of a ground floor (housing an assortment of businesses), a mezzanine, and nine residential floors (Tintillier, 1997: 66). It is in the northernmost of these buildings, which are set slightly back from the busy main road, where you'll find Hélène's apartment. A heritage plaque on the right-hand side of the *Muriel* building's entrance confirms that these structures are indeed known by the borrowed word "buildings", with the architect named as Pierre Vivien and the years of construction listed as 1951–1956. For his work on reconstructing the bombed-out working class areas surrounding the port, Vivien certainly earned his commemorative plaque, and more detail reveals the immense scale of his project:

> [T]he idea of replanning the fishing port of Boulogne had preceded wartime destruction and its liberation in September 1944, when only one-tenth of its housing remained habitable [...]. [...] These proposals remained at the heart of the reconstruction plan prepared by Pierre Vivien (1909–1999), a young architect originating from Amiens and a political ally of de Gaulle, who was appointed architect–planner for Boulogne early in 1945. After studying the town's history and physical site, [...] Vivien's project [...] also proposed four 11-storey apartment blocks along Quai Gambetta, which would require substantial *remembrement* [land consolidation] and drastically alter the appearance of that part of town. After much local debate, Vivien's wide-ranging plan for rebuilding Boulogne and reorganizing its major economic activity received approval in Paris in 1950. Combining a certain respect for tradition in the town center with notable innovation along the waterfront, it shaped the reconstruction of the town in the following decade. (Kirsch and Flint, 2011: 168–169)

Among the aforementioned grand hotels sited on Gambetta was the Folkestone, named for the English town which, for many years, was connected to Boulogne by cross-channel ferry, and in *Muriel* Hélène laments the loss of this establishment, sighing "poor Folkestone" as

The plaque on the *Muriel* building, February 2020.

she reminisces on the venue where she and Alphonse once spent a few happy days; one can sense that Hélène views the hotel as a symbol of her relationship with Alphonse: once beautiful, now ruined beyond repair (or, more accurately, it's now hard to believe it ever existed at all). Furthermore, as Hélène's current lover, Roland de Smoke, claims to own the hotel's salvaged marble staircase, the Folkestone forms a connection between her romances; all that's missing from this memory chain is Hélène's late husband, the seldom-spoken-of Gérard Aughain, whose first name is mentioned just once in the entire film.

While Pierre Vivien is to be commended for his work in transforming the rubble of WWII into a living, functioning city, it is obvious that his utilitarian designs, at least from an aesthetic standpoint, are no match for the majestic, glittering buildings which once lined Boulogne's seafront, but the pragmatic need to re-home so many people outweighed any artistic considerations. Daniel Tintillier notes how "the bombs destroyed everything" on Gambetta, including "one of the most beautiful casinos in France" (1997: 107). Contrast this with the casino's postwar replacement, which Robert Benayoun considered to be "pretty hideous" (2002: 137). In a move which demonstrates the evolving nature of the city, the casino frequented by Hélène in *Muriel* was itself razed to make way for Boulogne's huge, aforementioned aquarium, which opened in 1991. However, the city's perennial love of a good gambling hall ensured that Boulogne wouldn't be without one, and the present-day (and somewhat prettier) casino is now housed on the left bank of the Liane river, although at the time of writing this building, like much of its immediate vicinity, is undergoing remodeling.

With great symmetry, *Muriel* has two titles—the other being *The Time of Return*—and its setting has two distinct sides. While the *return* in the film's title could equally apply to the literal returns of

Muriel's "pretty hideous" casino, which was demolished in 1987.

both Bernard and Alphonse, it could also be a reference to the city both characters come back to, given that "new" Boulogne still carries very noticeable traces of its wartime trauma, and these scars mean that, in a sense, the reconstructed city is constantly forced to face up to the horror of WWII. There are a number of returns in *Muriel*, but the indistinct meaning of the English title is exacerbated when you consider that the film's original French title literally translates as *Muriel, or The Time of a Return*. The inclusion of the indefinite article makes quite a difference—but which particular return does the film's original title refer to?

Boulogne is a city composed of two very different halves which, much like the contrasting red and black pockets of the roulette wheel Hélène is so fond of, live side by side. It is "a reconstructed city, at once ancient and modern, where the past and the precarious future mingle inextricably" (ibid.: 132). It is exactly this suspended half-life

Boulogne's Boulevard Gambetta, pre-WWII. Note the Folkestone Hotel on the left.

that attracted Jean Cayrol and Alain Resnais to the city for the way in which it would inform their film's characters; an undamaged town, or one built completely anew, would not have serviced the filmmakers' needs. Just as the clocks in Hiroshima, the backdrop for Resnais' feature debut, stopped at 8:15 a.m. as the Enola Gay dropped its payload on the city, *Muriel*'s characters are similarly frozen in time; none of them are able to see how the past and future are pretty much the same, the main difference being that only the former is illuminated. Yet no-one in *Muriel* seems very interested in the future, preferring to focus on the past as the present bleeds out. An exception to this comes in the form of Bernard's cheerful, optimistic girlfriend Marie-Do, who is making firm plans to leave France for Uruguay.

As most of the characters in *Muriel* are stuck in a no man's land between past and present, they therefore serve as an extension of their surroundings. While such a state might just about work for a place, it is far from ideal for a person, and the very recognizable malaise which hangs over these characters is one which is rotting them from the inside out—even if it could quite easily pass for the human condition. Bernard, Hélène, Alphonse and the others "are always between two memories, between two times, between two passions, unstable, badly put, not knowing the limits of their existence" (Bounoure, 1962, as cited in Monaco, 1979: 87). Boulogne may well be "a ghost town"—just not in the traditional sense of the phrase (Benayoun, 2002: 132). *Muriel*'s characters certainly sync up with their surroundings, but that isn't to say that they're completely oblivious to this—at one point, an irate Françoise spits that Boulogne "feeds on memories", which is as much an admonishment of the other characters as it is a sign of her vexation with the town she's found herself in.

The stasis and inertia of *Muriel*'s characters sees Boulogne, rather like the titular building in Mark Z. Danielewski's novel *House of Leaves*, apparently reconfigure itself around them. Much of the city is in the midst of seemingly endless construction work presided over by Roland, who the bumptious Alphonse disparagingly refers to as "Mr. Demolition". Additionally, Boulogne–Tintelleries station, where Alphonse and Françoise arrived from Paris, suddenly stops serving France's capital. While many viewers will assume this to be a contrivance for the film, its basis lies in fact: 1962 was when

Boulogne–Tintelleries station, February 2020.

train services between Boulogne and Paris were transferred from Tintelleries to the new Boulogne–Ville station, which had been built to replace the one completely destroyed in the war. Despite its name, Boulogne–Ville is actually slightly farther from the city center than the pretty Tintelleries building, which has since been served by regional rail services and also suffered notable, albeit reversible, damage during the Battle of France.

During the fraught Sunday lunch that occurs late on in *Muriel*, the foursquare Ernest performs an impromptu, haunting rendition of Paul Colline's Jazz Age hit "Déja" ("Already"). Given all that's preceded this musical interlude, the song's message—that it's quite possible to be happy in the present on earth, but we instead opt to fear the future and/or dwell on the past—carries real bite. Ernest is a relative latecomer to the film, but even from our limited time with him it's clear that he, unlike the other main characters, is a pragmatist (albeit one who may once have had a dalliance with Hélène, who appears to instantly recognize him); as such, the words he sings aren't especially relevant to himself but do apply to the many distracted dreamers who populate both room and film. It's almost as if this uninvited guest, who could also be viewed as a Typhoid Mary, is holding a mirror up to Hélène, Bernard, Françoise and Alphonse, and this moment of reflective calm comes just before a mighty storm including, but not limited to, Ernest's revelations and Bernard's subsequent meltdown. Ernest seems immune to Boulogne's effects, but there's a sense that he is acutely aware of the city's influence over many of those sat around the dinner table.

Ernest's song functions as something approximating a disaster march for Cayrol and Resnais' characters, and the aftermath sees the dinner guests scatter in various directions. The home truths "Déja" contains pushes some of these people to the point of no return and, to draw an unfortunate parallel with Boulogne's wartime past, the result is as if someone has detonated a bomb in the apartment. This effect extends to behind the lens: Resnais' camera is finally, suddenly untethered, and just before the film comes to a close, we're treated to an extended, *Marienbad*-like tracking shot through Hélène's apartment. In its own way, this sequence feels as liberating as the one in which the young Antoine Doinel runs along the beach at the conclusion of Truffaut's *The 400 Blows*; finally, we can breathe.

As we've already established, the past six decades have seen Boulogne-sur-Mer become inseparable from Alain Resnais' *Muriel*, and it is fair to say that no other film has captured the mood and feel of the city in quite the same way. While *Muriel* is virtually unsurpassable as a snapshot of the two sides of postwar Boulogne, other movies have been filmed in the new city both before and since Resnais arrived there in the early 1960s: British comedy drama *A Day to Remember* (1953), which followed a group of Londoners on a day trip to Boulogne, was released less than a decade after the end of the war; crime novel adaptation *Room of Death/Melody's Smile* (*La chambre des morts*, 2007) used the city to good effect as a backdrop for its bleak serial killer story; musical documentary *We Did It on a Song* (*Chante ton bac d'abord*, 2014) followed a group of Boulogne high school students as they prepared for their final exams; and, most recently, crime caper *Rebelles* (2019) charted the escapades of three put-upon fish cannery workers who join forces after accidentally killing their sleazy boss.

There are some other examples, but on the whole the possibilities of Boulogne as a filmmaking location have rarely been fully exploited. The same is true for the rest of the Pas-de-Calais department in which Boulogne is situated, and in recent times only local filmmaker Bruno Dumont has made full use of the area's potential with works such as *Slack Bay*, *Joan of Arc* (*Jeanne*, 2019), and *L'il Quinquin* (*P'tit Quinquin*, 2014) and its sequel. Perhaps it doesn't really matter that Boulogne and its environs are frequently passed over by both tourists and filmmakers alike, as with *Muriel, or The Time of Return* Alain Resnais somehow managed to capture the soul of a distinctive city that rose from the ashes of war. One thing is certain: Boulogne without *Muriel* is now as unimaginable as *Muriel* without Boulogne.

The Question: *Muriel* and Torture In the Algerian War

Chapter Three

MURIEL **WAS WRITTEN** by Holocaust survivor Jean Cayrol, a notable author who, like Alain Resnais' previous screenwriters Marguerite Duras and Alain Robbe-Grillet, was associated with the avant-garde style of the *nouveau roman* (new novel). Given Resnais' auteur reputation, it's somewhat surprising to note that he only received credit for the writing of a handful of the many films he directed; while he generally made very wise decisions when it came to selecting screenwriters, Resnais nevertheless devoted a great deal of time to refining each of his films' screenplays. Cayrol and Resnais had previously collaborated on *Night and Fog*, which took an unblinking look at the WWII extermination camps its writer survived. The harrowing *Night and Fog* received great acclaim, with none other than François Truffaut considering the film to be deserving of the highest of praise:

> The effective war film is often the one in which the action begins after the war, when there is nothing but ruins and desolation everywhere: Rossellini's *Germany Year Zero* (1947) and, above all, Alain Resnais' *Nuit et brouillard* [*Night and Fog*], the greatest film ever made. (Lopate, 2003)

In *Muriel*, Cayrol again tapped into the horrors of war, this time taking the specter of WWII and grafting on an additional layer concerning the Algerian Revolution; the conflict had concluded just a few months before production began on *Muriel* and was therefore still in the French news when the film was released into cinemas. *Muriel* carries a heavy load: the weight of *two* wars bears down on it, as do traumata both personal and national. While both WWII and the Hélène–Alphonse relationship inform the story of *Muriel*, it is true to say that these events are firmly in the film's rear-view (not that *Muriel* cares to look in any other direction). Yet the war in Algeria was a raw, almost current problem for both *Muriel*'s characters (especially Bernard) and viewers. Bernard's story is in effect retold in Chicago band Rise Against's 2008 track "Hero of War", in which a young man enlists in the army and, despite his initial protestations, subsequently joins his colleagues in beating and torturing a man they've captured. The song ends with the soldier, now numbed and disconnected, returning home from the unnamed war.

No-one in *Muriel* knows how to deal with the Algerian War's legacy: Bernard obsesses over his part in the conflict, while Alphonse dismisses Bernard's military service, asking, "What did he do in Algeria, other than occupy it? Later, he'll learn the real meaning of war". We should not forget that the conceited Alphonse, who describes himself as an "influential" figure in Algiers, claims to have run a café in the city, which, even if true, is hardly the same as Bernard's experience of Algeria. These two characters are at the opposite ends of a spectrum on which most opt to settle in the middle, and the others in *Muriel* acknowledge the Algerian War without daring to scratch the surface. It is in this way that *Muriel* acts as a microcosm of the France of the time, in which there were some extremes of opinion regarding Algeria, yet many didn't know how to react in the aftermath of a complex situation which was a direct consequence of France's colonial meddling.

It is worth taking a few moments to provide some context regarding the Algerian War. France invaded Algeria in 1830, and the first three decades of the conquest saw a terrible massacre in which up to one-third of Algeria's population of three million were killed by the occupying forces. In 1848, Algeria was declared to be an integral part of France, and this status was retained until more than halfway through the twentieth century. This last detail is important as it meant, from a legal standpoint, that Algeria was as French as Paris, Marseille, Lyon—or even Boulogne. Algeria was formed of three French departments—Oran, Alger and Constantine—populated by both indigenous Muslims and those of French (and other European) origin, with the latter gaining both most of the power and the soubriquet *Pieds-Noir* (black feet). In November 1956, the front cover image of a Belgian surrealist journal highlighted the concept of French Algeria in a novel, striking manner:

> Although untitled, the image is easy to recognize. Vaguely hexagonal, in black ink against a white background, it represents France. [...] What makes this image remarkable is the names next to each dot: "Algiers," next to the point that should be Paris; "Constantine" instead of Marseilles; "Oran" instead of Lyon and "Bône" in place of Lille. [...] Marcel Mariën's work captures something that most analyses of "the Algerian War" avoid engaging. In it, Algeria is shaped like France, making visual the catch phrase of those who rejected Algerian independence, "L'Algérie, c'est la France" [Algeria is France]. This does more than point out how ridiculous the concept is: it also suggests that what we know as France has Algeria written all over it. This would have seemed dubious, maybe troubling, to most of the journal's audience when "La dernière carte" [the last map] was published in 1956. It would become difficult even to imagine after 1962, when [...] the now obvious moniker "the Hexagon" began to be widely used to refer to France. (Shepard, 2006: 269)

Algerians of all origins fought for France in WWII, but in 1954 the *Front de libération nationale* (National Liberation Front, or FLN) called on all Muslim Algerians to rise up in order to restore the Algerian state. France, having just lost Indochina, was determined to hold on to Algeria and deployed hundreds of thousands of troops to fight FLN forces. Yet the French authorities were in no rush to admit to the gravity of the situation, and mainland France was kept largely in the dark regarding developments in the colony.

This all changed in 1958 when, with the conflict entering its fourth year, France's Fourth Republic fell; at the beginning of the following year, President Coty stepped down and Resistance hero Charles de Gaulle was returned to power. It was during this period that France's army began to exert control in Algeria, and a French victory looked to be in sight. While the French gained military superiority, "they lost the war of ideas, that of propaganda and persuasion, and as a result relinquished to Algeria its independence" (Sparks, 2011: 1). After the disappointments of both WWII and Indochina, France was doomed to a third consecutive defeat and the cumulative effect impacted on its global image. The tide of public opinion turned for several reasons, not least because the violence spilled over into mainland France, and in 1961 de Gaulle proposed a referendum on Algeria's future, in which all of France (including the three Algerian departments) was eligible to vote. Around 75 percent of the electorate opted for Algerian independence, with hostilities concluding in 1962. Over the next two years, a majority of the million *Pieds-Noirs*, having been given the option of *la valise ou le cercueil* (the suitcase or the coffin), unsurprisingly fled to mainland France. Most *harkis* (indigenous Algerian Muslims who served in the French Army), despite their loyalty to France during the conflict, were denied such an opportunity and were left to face lynchings and/or the wrath of the FLN:

> Euphoria at independence was mixed with a basic desire for revenge and with the FLN leadership exercising little control over the grassroots it was local leaders who made the running, their pent-up fury eventually exploding into a full-scale quest to root out the enemies of the people. Now, in an explicit inversion of colonial power, the hunters became the hunted as the *harkis* were subjected to every conceivable form of torment. Angry onlookers hurled abuse while men, women and children were beaten, tortured and killed and this bestial maltreatment had a strong ritualistic element. Some men were castrated, some were buried alive, others were dressed up as women and paraded in the streets—in each case the intention was to insult their manhood and underline their separation from the nation. (Evans, et al., 2002: 127)

The Algerian War, which has frequently been referred to as a "War Without a Name" due to the French government's steadfast refusal to recognize it as a war (although it eventually did so in 1999), rapidly descended into a conflict in which the practice of torture was widespread. From the perspective of the French authorities, the fact that France wasn't participating in a war meant that the usual rules of engagement did not apply: no war, ergo no war crimes. Given that Algeria was part of France, it could also have been argued that the conflict was actually a civil war, or that the French authorities were dealing with fifth columnists.

Under the pretext that they were dealing with terrorists, the French employed a variety of torture methods in their attempts to extract information from anyone suspected of aiding the FLN. As those captured and interrogated weren't considered to be prisoners of war, the rules of the Geneva Convention were not adhered to. Torture techniques were numerous, and on the milder end included sleep deprivation, experimental truth serums, and the use of the notorious *gégène* (Tucker Telephone) to administer electric shocks. Various euphemisms were introduced to mask the nature of the acts: torture with electricity was known as "rock 'n' roll"; prolonged immersion in water was coded as "breaststroke"; exposure to temperatures just short of 150° was referred to as "sunbathing"; and, the end of the line for the many prisoners too damaged by the other forms of torture—which itself was covered by the umbrella term "forceful interrogation"—came in the form of executions veiled as "wood duty" (ibid.: 104). As the war escalated, so did the frequency of summary executions and, during the year-long Battle of Algiers, paratroopers from France's 10th Parachute Division carried out "death flights", in which victims were flown over the sea and subsequently dropped to their deaths. The name of paratrooper commander Marcel Bigeard was incorporated into the chilling term given to those who suffered this terrible fate: *crevettes Bigeard* (Bigeard's shrimps).

Before we come to examine how *Muriel* deals with the subject of torture as implemented in the Algerian War, it is worth considering how Jean-Luc Godard's *Le petit soldat* depicted the practice. As mentioned in the introduction, Godard's second film (after *Breathless*) was made in 1960 but sat on the shelf for three years at the behest of the French authorities, who reportedly threatened Swiss national Godard's visa status. *Le petit soldat* was only released once the Algerian War had ended, and although the film first graced cinemas in the same year as *Muriel*, the two films' treatment of the same subject could hardly have been more different, although there is a curious coincidence present in that a reel-to-reel tape recorder plays a critical role in each film's dénouement.

Le petit soldat, which translates as *The Little Soldier*, concerns Bruno Forestier, a French Army deserter who's currently living in Switzerland. Forestier is working for a murky branch of French intelligence and has been tasked with assassinating a Swiss radio host believed to have links to the FLN. Before Bruno can carry out his mission, he meets and falls in love with the beautiful Véronica Dreyer, and the couple decides to leave for Brazil. Forestier is captured and brutally tortured by FLN agents, but manages to escape and still hopes to leave the country with Véronica. On the understanding that he will receive a pair of diplomatic passports, Forestier shoots the radio host in the street. However, Bruno's superiors discover that Véronica has ties to the FLN, and she's tortured to death.

It is not difficult to see why *Le petit soldat* was initially banned in France—a full sixty years on, the film still manages to disturb with its extended torture sequence, in which Michel Subor's Forestier is burned with a lighter, shocked by electrodes, and waterboarded; at least one of these torments—the third—is most definitely unsimulated. Yet it was the notion that France was involved in a dirty war, one which—according to *Le petit soldat*'s Véronica—it would lose on account of its lack of conviction, that really raised the hackles of the French government, who were no doubt left further unimpressed by the heavy allusion that Forestier was working for *La Main rouge* (the Red Hand), the shadowy organization created by French foreign intelligence in order to eliminate FLN leaders and supporters. By the time *Le petit soldat* appeared on France's cinema screens, it was widely felt that its moment had somewhat passed, but there is no denying that the impact of the film, had it been released as planned, would have been considerable. As it happened, the French public didn't need *Le petit soldat* to alert them to the use of torture in the Algerian War, as news of the practice trickled through to the mainland as the war was in progress, thus bolstering the move toward Algerian independence.

Perhaps the most surprising aspect of *Le petit soldat*, which introduced its director's oft-quoted maxim that "cinema is truth twenty-four times per second", is that Godard, a filmmaker who rarely sits on the fence, presented a fairly even-handed account. Crucially, Godard highlighted how torture was used by both sides in the conflict, although only the punishment meted out by the FLN was depicted onscreen, with the details of Véronica's torture and subsequent demise left to the viewer's imagination. There is some nuance present in the film, given that the war is (and was) often "simplified into two polarized narratives where on one reading the French army are sadistic torturers waging a 'dirty war' and, on the other the National Liberation Front (FLN) are fanatical terrorists inflicting savagery upon defenceless civilians" (ibid.: 2).

Le petit soldat saw Godard repeat the same trick he'd performed in *Breathless*, which was to incorporate the unwitting public into a climactic scene in which a man is shot dead in the street. Just as Jean-Paul Belmondo's death rattle at the close of *Breathless* was captured in front of startled Parisian onlookers, the blank fired by Michel Subor at the end of *Le petit soldat* saw the actor pursued through the streets of Geneva by members of the Swiss public, who were convinced they'd just witnessed a real-life shooting (Brody, 2008). This scene, coupled with the very real torture inflicted on Subor, sees *Le petit soldat* achieve a rare sense of realism, one that is only slightly negated by Godard's decision to go with post-sync dubbing.

In Godard's film, there is a brief glimpse (and excerpt) of Henri Alleg's critical text *La Question* (*The Question*), an account of its writer's arrest and torture by the 10th Paratrooper Division. London-born Alleg was an Algiers newspaper editor whose anti-colonialist stance had attracted the attention of the authorities; although he evaded capture for some time, Alleg was eventually arrested in June 1957 at the home of math professor Maurice Audin. Although no charges were brought against Alleg, he was subjected to one month of extreme torture, and experienced waterboarding, burning, injections of sodium pentothal, being hung upside-down, and electric shocks from more than one type of *gégène*. Alleg was threatened with execution on more than one occasion, and thought he heard his friend Audin—who had also been arrested—being murdered (in 2018 , France's President Macron acknowledged that Maurice Audin had indeed died under torture). Despite these cruelties, Alleg steadfastly refused to cooperate with the Paras, and eventually they gave up and shoved him on to the massively overcrowded Barberousse prison, where he wrote *La Question*. Alleg's lawyers smuggled the manuscript out of the building, and the book was published in mainland France in February 1958. One month after its publication, *La Question* was banned. Before it could be seized, however, it sold some 60,000 copies, which constituted most of its initial print run, so the genie was well and truly out of the bottle regarding France's use of torture in Algeria. It's not difficult to see why *La Question* sickened and horrified a large section of the French public:

> Rolling my shirt into a ball, Ja—— stuck it in my mouth and the ordeal started again. I clenched the material between my teeth with all my might and almost found relief in it. Suddenly, I felt like a wild animal had torn the flesh from my body. Still smiling above me, Ja—— had attached the pincer to my penis. The tremors that shook me were so strong that the straps that held my ankles came loose. They stopped to tie them up and continued. Soon the lieutenant took over from Ja——. He had stripped a wire from the pincers and fastened it across the width of my chest. I was completely shaken by increasingly violent nervous shocks, and the session continued. I had been sprayed with cold water to further strengthen the intensity of the current and between every two spasms, I trembled with cold. Around me, sitting on the packing cases, Cha—— and his friends were draining bottles of beer. I chewed on my gag to escape the cramp which contorted my whole body. In vain. (Alleg, 1958: 44–45)

As Alain Resnais would have been very aware of the censorship travails of both *La Question* and *Le petit soldat* as he prepared to film *Muriel*, he must have anticipated similar problems. As Godard's film was only granted a theatrical release as production was wrapping on *Muriel*, Resnais was really only able to use *Le petit soldat* as a bellwether for what *wasn't* acceptable when it came to onscreen depictions of the

Henri Alleg in 2008.

Algerian War. In the blunt, direct *Le petit soldat*, torture was dealt with both explicitly and implicitly in the respective cases of Forestier and Véronica. This does lend a certain imbalance to proceedings, but it nevertheless provides a small clue as to how *Muriel*, albeit in a much more sophisticated manner, would tackle this thorny subject, and Resnais realized that there was another, third way in which torture could be represented on film. In Resnais' movie, just as in Godard's, the torture and murder of a female victim by French forces is spoken of but not shown. The Muriel of the title is dead before the movie begins, yet her death is at the very core of the film. In a move that pushes the limits of the perversity of this setup, it turns out that Muriel may not even be the woman's real name, and Bernard, who brought the specter of Muriel back to Boulogne, questions as much in his account of her death (see below). Resnais had to work out the logistics of how to make Muriel's death carry significant emotional weight; Godard had no such problems when it came to engendering sympathy for Véronica, as the audience had just spent most of an entire film with the character. Cayrol and Resnais solved this by going against the old writing (and filmmaking) tenet "show, don't tell", and included a sequence in which Bernard described Muriel's end in some detail:

> They told me her name was Muriel. I don't know why, but it didn't seem to be her real name. There were five of us around her. We were chatting. She had to talk before nightfall. Robert stooped and turned her over. Muriel groaned. She put her arm over her eyes. We let go of her. She fell like a sack. That's when it started again. We pulled her to the middle of the hangar for a better view. Robert kicked her. He took a flashlight and shone it on her. Her lips were swollen, full of foam. We tore off her clothes. We tried to put her on a chair, but she fell down. One arm was sort of twisted. We had to get it over with. Even if she had wanted to speak, she couldn't have. I joined in. Muriel was groaning as she received the slaps. The palms of my hands were burning. Muriel's hair was all wet. Robert lit a cigarette. He approached her. She screamed. Her gaze fixed on me. Why me? She closed her eyes and started vomiting. Robert backed away, disgusted. I left them all. At night I went back to see her. I lifted the tarp. It was as if she had spent a long time in the water… like a split bag of potatoes… with blood all over her body and her hair… burns on her chest. Muriel's eyes weren't closed. It almost didn't matter to me, maybe

didn't even affect me at all. The next morning, before the salute to colors, Robert had disposed of her. (Cayrol, 1963: 89–90)

Bernard's observation that the dead Muriel's eyes were open ties in with a couple of odd moments elsewhere in the film: one in which Bernard, during the first dinner scene and for no apparent reason, sports a pair of novelty glasses with wide eyes painted on them, the other when the same character, lying in bed with Marie-Do, instructs his startled girlfriend not to close her eyes. The second of these incidents occurs less than two minutes before Bernard begins recounting the details of Muriel's murder. His description of Muriel's sorry fate is sufficiently harrowing, which proves that we don't actually need to *see* the violence to be appalled by it. Even if censorial constraints hadn't been in place, Resnais' less-is-more approach is extremely effective and is certainly preferable to watching Muriel's degradation and murder. Even without congruent images, this stretch of dialogue is undeniably shocking, especially for a film from the early 1960s, and one suspects that it pushed the limits of what was deemed acceptable. The challenge for Alain Resnais, having presumably decided that an audio description of torture *would* be permitted, was how to effectively frame such dialogue in the film. As both a main character and one of the perpetrators, Bernard was always going to be the natural choice to relate the story of Muriel's murder, but what to show onscreen, given that images of a similar graphic intensity were completely out of the question and, conversely, a milder, diluted depiction of Muriel's torture would make little sense?

Resnais circumvented this problem by having grainy home movie-style footage of French soldiers in Algeria accompany Bernard's spoken account of this terrible incident. The images in this sequence are mostly benign, and include the soldiers engaging in a variety of activities, such as practicing on a firing range, shaking the hands of Algerian children, digging trenches, and swimming. Only the very end of Bernard's lens-flared film hints at a more sinister side to the military presence, as two soldiers angrily kick down a door. Who or what is behind the door is unknown, as the camera tilts up and the film comes to an abrupt close. While the bulk of the images show good-natured

Muriel's Hélène (Delphine Seyrig) investigates Bernard's workroom.

troops and are therefore in stark contrast to what's being described, the distressed, scratchy, verité-style amateur film appears completely authentic, which in turn has the effect of making what we're hearing *feel* much more real, and we easily join the dots between the French military and Muriel's murder.

As this scene forces the viewer to play out Muriel's torture in their head, the end result is far more troubling than anything the special effects of the day might have conjured up. It's a bravura sequence, one largely borne of the necessity of sidestepping censorial wrath, and its terrible power lies in the dissonance between what is seen and what is heard. As this scene begins almost exactly halfway through *Muriel*, it stands as both the literal and figurative centerpiece of the film. Unsurprisingly, the 8 mm film has no soundtrack, but the whir of the projector is clearly audible; as is later revealed, Bernard possesses what we can assume to be an audio recording of Muriel's torture and murder, but he opts not to use this to augment his narration, presumably because it lacks the safety buffer its owner so desperately needs. Bernard may be obsessed with Muriel, but he has no desire to make such direct contact with her memory, as doing so would shatter the illusion he has so carefully constructed. There is really only one moment in *Muriel* that lacks subtlety, which occurs when Bernard is shown riding a white horse (which looks a lot like a Boulonnais, or White Marble Horse) in the countryside on the outskirts of Boulogne, and this imagery rather overplays the notion of Bernard recasting himself as the white knight in Muriel's story.

Bernard's account makes it plain that poor Muriel had endured more than one of the tortures as outlined earlier, with cigarette burns and water immersion among the torments inflicted on the unfortunate prisoner. It is also quite clear that Muriel has been severely beaten to the point of disfigurement, but while Cayrol's (and by extension Bernard's) description tells us that Muriel is stripped of her clothing, it stops short of mentioning sexual assault, although that is what we tacitly understand from this detail. This highlights yet another form of torture which was employed by French troops against their female Algerian prisoners, and Marnia Lazreg notes that "[a]lthough rape could take place without torture, torture seldom took place without rape" (2008: 160, as cited in McMahon, 2016: 227). It is quite possible that the torture of Muriel is based on the real-life case of Djamila Boupacha, a young Algerian woman arrested in 1960 on suspicion of planting a bomb in an Algiers café. Boupacha was subjected to various tortures including brutal sexual violence, and she eventually confessed to the crime she was accused of. Unlike the fictional Muriel, however, Boupacha survived her ordeal. While she was sentenced to death for the crime, Boupacha's execution had not been carried out by the time Algeria achieved its independence, and an amnesty was declared for all offenses committed during the conflict. Of course, such clemency extended to all on both sides, so the likes of French intelligence chief Paul Aussaresses—who openly admitted to personally liquidating two dozen FLN members—and Marcel Bigeard were granted immunity. The amnesty chillingly informs *Muriel*, too, although this is never made clear in the film: regardless of what they did to Muriel in Algeria, both Bernard and Robert are beyond legal reproach.

Although the description of torture in *Muriel* is as upsetting as it is effective, some were of the opinion that Alain Resnais

Djamila Boupacha in 2017.

operated comfortably within censorial limits; furthermore, not everyone felt that the film adequately addressed the burning issues of the day:

> Resnais's film has often been judged untimely in its failure to engage directly with the immediate events of the Algerian War [...]. For some critics, this failure crystallizes in the film's refusal to represent Muriel—absent from image and sound, Muriel is neither seen

nor heard; we know nothing of her life beyond the event of her torture; we never witness events from Muriel's point of view. Nor does the film appear to engage with the military and political realities of the Algerian War itself [...]. Though censorship in France at the time of *Muriel*'s release limited representation of the Algerian War [...], it has also been suggested that such restrictions were perhaps not obstructive enough to warrant the degree of narrative ellipsis adopted by Resnais's film. (ibid.: 220)

The above points raise two pertinent questions: Does *Muriel* really need to be any more graphic? Does the film really skirt around the issue of the Algerian War? The short answer to both, I think, is no. We have already considered how the viewer's imagination will almost certainly outstrip any visual depiction of Muriel's torture, if indeed such a spectacle was to be permitted. This in turn raises another question: would the prolonged, grueling torture sequence in *Le petit soldat* have been allowed if Véronica was the victim? Regarding the film's level of engagement with the Algerian War, it is true that *Muriel* essentially shows just one side of the conflict's aftermath, and as the film "solely expos[es] the experiences of the French soldier and civilian, it follows that its true investment is in representing its survivors rather than its victims" (Quinan, 2016: 19). Yet it is perhaps not inappropriate to consider that the reason why *Muriel* doesn't fully face up to the conflict is simply because France couldn't address its past. If France is *Muriel* writ large, then it shouldn't be too surprising to discover that country and film share the same problems.

While *Muriel*'s characters look conspicuously to the past, their memories are, for the most part, quite selective. Laura McMahon notes how "the fictional crises of *Muriel* [...] are indicative of a wider historical reality [...] that is melancholically resistant to memorialization, in that it perpetually calls into question the mournful memory-work of the nation-state" (2016: 221). France, like the other western European nations that once colonized large chunks of the globe, tends to view its colonial history through a prism, and the individuals in *Muriel* exhibit the same tendency when looking back on the events of their lives. Of course, in 1963 the wounds inflicted by the Algerian War were raw and open, but they ran alongside some deep, festering ones dating back to WWII:

> [R]eminding us of Algeria's role in the nation's memory of Vichy, both Hélène and Alphonse are prone to irrational fits when one's narrative of events is threatened by the other's version. Yet nothing poses a greater threat to the "climate of deliberate amnesia" exemplified by Hélène and Alphonse—if not the inhabitants of Boulogne in general—than Bernard and his "accumulation of proofs." Bernard's presence evokes Algeria, and that particular element of Algeria which [...] resurrected the darkest memories of France's collaborationist history: torture. (Croombs, 2010)

Essentially, Hélène and Alphonse must always remember to forget, and Bernard's ceaseless investigation, despite its amateur-hour quality, does little to put neither his stepmother nor her old flame at ease. Bernard's attempts to gather evidence are always directed at others and never at himself, and as such he has more or less absolved himself from his part in the torture and murder of Muriel. To varying extents, most of us do exactly the same as Hélène, Alphonse and Bernard, and to be human is to constantly reshape and edit the narrative of our own pasts. With this in mind, why should a nation be any different? The answer lies in the notion of collective, as opposed to individual, responsibility, yet countries are often loath to examine their unadorned history. As Aaron Kerner notes, "Casting off the yoke of memory (or history) is how we generally negotiate guilt, or actually more precisely responsibility for the past" (Pollock and Silverman, 2015: 116). Vichy France sits in the Gallic consciousness about as comfortably as Joan of Arc fits into an Anglo-Saxon narrative: which is to say, not very. In France's case, there is a further complication in that the Algerian War directly tarnished some of the nation's better memories of WWII; high-profile military men such as Bigeard, Aussaresses and General Jacques Massu had fought for de Gaulle's Free France during the Second World War, but these heroes became villains once their torturous tactics in Algeria were exposed, thus diminishing their anti-Nazi efforts in the eyes of much of the French public. As Shakespeare's Antony put it: "The evil that men do lives after them. The good is oft interred with their bones" (*JC*. 3.2.81–82).

Then there are those who achieved the unenviable feat of disgracing themselves in both wars, with a particular case in point being that of Maurice Papon who, after the longest trial in French history, was eventually convicted of war crimes in 1998. During the Second World War, Papon served as secretary general of the Regional Prefecture in Bordeaux, which formed part of Vichy France.

Plaque commemorating the Paris massacre of 1961.

Throughout the conflict, Papon collaborated with the Nazis, and under his watch more than 1500 Jews were deported to extermination camps. Papon later became Paris' police chief, and in October 1961 he ordered his officers to attack a pro-FLN demonstration that was taking place in the city; a massacre ensued as protestors were beaten, fired upon, and flung into the Seine. It is still not known how many died—a commemorative plaque simply states *nombreux* (many)—but the dozens of bodies floating in the river were both evidence of the mass drownings and a terrible marker of the police brutality instigated by Papon. The image above, taken in 2007, was first shared with a description (please see Appendix C) that lays the blame squarely on the chief of police. Many victims were thrown from the Pont Saint-Michel in Paris' city center, and shortly after the massacre a chilling scrawl of graffiti appeared on the side of the bridge: *ici on noie les Algériens* (here we drown Algerians).

It is doubtful if torture can ever be depicted on film in a way that could be considered to be completely accurate, and representation of the practice tends to be more effective in purely narrative film. In works such as *Saw* (2004), *Hostel* (2005) and their myriad sequels and copies, we can generally wince our way through something when we know it isn't real—no matter how accomplished the special effects might be; more importantly, we know such stories have no basis in reality. In this regard, *Muriel* occupies an unusual space as it is a work of fiction, yet it describes a practice we know had become commonplace during the Algerian War; of course, *Le petit soldat* is similarly anomalous, blurring the lines via its combination of a fictional framework with unsimulated torture analogous to that which occurred during the Algerian conflict.

Films which recreate, that is to say *fake*, documented acts of torture are significantly more problematic than either *Muriel* or the likes of *Saw*, because while we know such events actually took place, there is quite naturally a significant shortfall between what we're watching and what the very real victim experienced, which was by no means limited to their physical pain. While we should be thankful for this gap, it nevertheless proves that the cinematic representation of "real" torture is a somewhat futile exercise, as it can never replicate that subjective experience. As such, the act will always be diluted; "however 'authentic' the image, it remains a distortion of life" (Vogel, 1974, as cited in Kerekes and Slater, 2016). Few, if any, well-adjusted people wish or need to see intensely graphic reconstructions of real torture sessions, and Kristine Chick is quite right to query if we can "better understand events as traumatic as torture by seeing them acted out on-screen? Or are these essentially *inexprimable* [inexpressible], as [former *Cahiers* editor] Jean-Louis Comolli has argued. Are torture and death ('Muriel') absent just because we don't see them ('her')?" (2011: 61).

In sharp contrast to the way in which *Muriel* chooses to deal with torture, *La Question* (1977) vainly attempts to adapt Henri Alleg's eponymous autobiographical text. Laurent Heynemann's film—his debut—is a well-meaning work that isn't a *bad* film per se, but it plays along the lines of a rote wartime thriller, one which completely fails to capture the immediate, terrifying nature of Alleg's writing. In essence, the book is virtually unfilmable, being as it is a litany of agony that puts the reader firmly in the writer's position. Most damningly, the entire film is less effective than just one passage in the book; such an example can be found in the earlier quoted description of Alleg's experience with the *gégène*, but his account of being waterboarded is equally disturbing:

> When everything was ready, he said to me, "When you want to speak, all you have to do is wiggle your fingers". And he turned on the tap. The rag soaked quickly. Water was flowing everywhere: in my mouth, in my nose, all over my face. But for a while I could still take a few sips of air. I was trying to contract the gullet, absorb as little water as possible and resist asphyxiation by holding on as long as I could to the air in my lungs. But I couldn't last more than a few moments. I had the impression of drowning, and a terrible agony, that of death itself, took possession of me. In spite of myself, all the muscles of my body struggled uselessly to tear me away from choking, and the fingers of my two hands shook uncontrollably. "That's it! He's going to talk," said a voice. (1958: 48–49)

Alleg's book brings us uncomfortably close to the author's experiences, but the film that shares its name proves to be perfectly tolerable viewing, which is presumably not its intended effect given that it's based on a text which relays the horrors of wall-to-wall torture. At just over sixty pages, the highly concentrated *La Question* could be read in roughly the same time it takes to watch the film, but the book plunges us headlong into a nightmare that the film fails to replicate, which has the unfortunate effect of lessening Alleg's experiences in the eyes of the viewer; it's a serviceable film, but a terrible adaptation.

The movie of *La Question* unwisely opts to widen the scope of the book, opening it up to include scenes set in a sun-drenched Algiers where life, in the main and despite the turmoil, continues. In doing so, it instantly negates the claustrophobic, relentless intensity of the book, most of which takes place in the dank building where Henri Alleg was tortured; the necessarily one-paced *La Question* is one work which really does not need light and shade. The approach employed by the filmmakers largely misses the point of the text, although there is one excellent addition in the form of a piece of dialogue given to the beleaguered Secretary General of the Police: "I didn't escape a Nazi concentration camp just to condone the same thing here". This echoes the sentiments of Jean-Paul Sartre in his preface to *La Question*, in which he pointedly observed that "fifteen years are enough to transform victims into executioners" (ibid.: 28). This reversal of roles did not go unnoticed by the French public and, given the torture of captured French Resistance members during WWII, "many French people found it intolerable that liberated France would also engage in torture. The revelations of torture by the French government now made many French citizens question the cost of holding on to Algeria" (Brody, 2008).

More than three decades on from Heynemann's sadly misguided film, his wife Caroline Huppert adapted Djamila Boupacha's story for the screen with the TV movie *Pour Djamila* (2011), which was based on a book by Sartre's longtime partner Simone de Beauvoir and Boupacha's lawyer Gisèle Halimi. Prior to the book's publication, de Beauvoir had already written a controversial article titled *Pour Djamila Boupacha*, which was published in French newspaper *Le Monde*. In a parallel with *La Question*, de Beauvoir's article proves far more disturbing than anything contained in *Pour Djamila*, although Huppert's film is an affecting work which owes much to the excellent performances of Hafsia Herzi and Marina Hands, who respectively play Boupacha and Halimi. The *Le Monde* article, which memorably opens with, "The most scandalous thing about scandal is that you get used to it", details how Boupacha's torturers "attached electrodes to the breasts with Scotch tape, then applied them to the legs, groin, sex, face. Punches and cigarette burns alternated with electrical torture. Then Djamila was hung […] over a bathtub and submerged several times" (de Beauvoir, 1960). Djamila was quoted in the piece, and explained how she "was given the torture of the bottle; it is the most atrocious of sufferings; after having tied me in a special position, the neck of a bottle was thrust into my stomach. I screamed and lost consciousness for, I think, two days" (ibid.).

Caroline Huppert in 2018.

De Beauvoir's article makes for harrowing if necessary reading, and that's before one learns that the writer was forced to substitute the milder "stomach" for another part of the female anatomy. The "torture of the bottle" was a grim holdover from the war in Indochina and is depicted, fairly graphically, in Huppert's film; few victims survived this particular cruelty, given its high chance of perforating the intestines. While there is material in *Pour Djamila* that is admittedly more upsetting than anything presented in the film of *La Question*, one suspects that this otherwise solid film (and by extension the viewer) would be better served by the omission of its few torture scenes. As Alain Resnais proved with *Muriel*, a description of torture needn't be accompanied by an illustrative flashback, as such a device often works to the detriment of the point being made.

From the examples given in this chapter, we might conclude that direct representations of torture in the Algerian War don't really work on film, yet are significantly more potent in prose form. There are other art forms that also fare better than the moving image when it comes to depicting torture, and in 1978 the Scott Walker-penned track "The Electrician" appeared on The Walker Brothers' final album *Nite Flights*. This song sees Walker edge further away from pop and toward the avant-garde of his later recordings as it wraps an ominous soundscape around its description of the work of a CIA torturer. In terms of imparting a mood, the six-minute "The Electrician" greatly outstrips any of the films discussed in this chapter (*Muriel* aside), and the song's eroticization of torture moves the debate into an area that would almost certainly make *Muriel's* Bernard most uncomfortable.

France's longstanding devotion to the *bande dessinée* (graphic novel, or comic) has meant that another outlet exists in which the war's more extreme aspects can be conveyed. Given France's problematic relationship with the Algerian War, graphic novels can provide an opportunity for younger readers—who may not be overly inclined to read the likes of *La Question* or *Djamila Boupacha*—to become acquainted with a history that may have been substantially airbrushed before it is presented in schools. In *The Algerian War in French-Language Comics*, Jennifer Howell observes how:

> French schoolchildren [...] are seldom exposed to graphic images of violence and war in the classroom. [...] [T]extbook images of the Algerian War typically show de Gaulle, demonstrations orchestrated by Algeria's European population, and the Pied-Noir exodus. French cartoonists [...] often represent violence and taboo topics in their albums, including mutilation, torture, rape, summary executions, and the French army's scorched-earth policy. Comics deliberately recycle violent images in order to unearth dark periods of France's national past, and episodes that have yet to securely anchor themselves in collective memory such as the October 17, 1961 massacre in Paris. (2015: 67)

In its own way, and as far as narrative cinema is concerned, *Muriel* contains what is arguably the best representation of torture in the Algerian War simply by virtue of omitting any visual depiction of the practice. While this may sound contradictory, images tend to quantify and dictate the extent of a given horror, whereas the human imagination imposes no such boundaries. Bernard's description of the torture and murder of the fictional Muriel achieves a rare verisimilitude, and it lingers in the mind long after the onscreen reconstructions of Alleg and Boupacha's torments have faded.

The Star: Delphine Seyrig In *Muriel*

Chapter Four

IT WAS WAY BACK in 1990 when cancer claimed the lives of my two favorite actresses: Juliet Berto and Delphine Seyrig. The doe-eyed Berto remains best known for her collaborations with Jean-Luc Godard and Jacques Rivette, and she became the female face of the French New Wave (her frequent co-star Jean-Pierre Léaud was very much the movement's poster boy). Berto was just forty-two when she succumbed to breast cancer and, a mere nine months later, lung cancer would kill Seyrig at the comparatively old age of fifty-eight. While Seyrig and Berto contributed much to cinema during their combined century on this earth, both still had a great deal to offer had their lives not been cut short. The two actresses boasted very different styles and never starred alongside each other, although Berto featured in the Seyrig-directed *Be Pretty and Shut Up* (*Sois belle et tais-toi*, 1981). Berto would also move behind the camera, and in the 1980s would direct three quietly impressive features in *Neige* (1981), *Cap Canaille* (1983) and *Havre* (1986), from which we can extrapolate that she would have continued to enjoy a successful career as a director for many years.

If Juliet Berto became synonymous with the New Wave, it is perhaps not too much of a stretch to claim that Delphine Seyrig, to an admittedly lesser extent, came to represent the Left Bank group of directors, given that she worked with both Alain Resnais and a number of his Left Bank associates, including *Hiroshima mon amour* writer Marguerite Duras, Jacques Demy, and Agnès Varda. While Seyrig's body of work spanned way beyond Left Bank films, it is surprising to note that she appeared in just one film directed by a member of the *Cahiers* set: François Truffaut's *Stolen Kisses* (*Baisers volés*, 1968), which may just be its director's best film; the following year, the actress reportedly contributed some uncredited voiceover work to Truffaut's *Mississippi Mermaid* (*La sirene du Mississippi*, 1969). In *Stolen Kisses*, the second feature film in Truffaut's Antoine Doinel cycle—*The 400 Blows* and the short *Antoine and Colette* (*Antoine et Colette*, 1962) had preceded it—Seyrig is terrific in the role of Fabienne Tabard, the older woman who catches the eye of the film's protagonist, but a letter to Truffaut revealed the actress' dissatisfaction with her performance:

> 'I very quickly realized how little I contributed to *Stolen Kisses*', she later wrote to Truffaut, though he was sincerely captivated by her elegance and presence. 'I'm in despair that I'm so lacking in inventiveness; Jean-Pierre Léaud impressed me—and everyone, I think—with his charm and freedom of movement and speech in front of the camera. You see, he has exactly the qualities I wanted to have. His freedom with words, his ease in improvising, this is what I would most like to acquire. And he has this naturally. I wish I had been more equal to the task.' (de Baecque and Toubiana, 1999: 234–235).

Anyone who has had the pleasure of watching *Stolen Kisses* will almost certainly be taken aback by Seyrig's criticism of her own work, as in Truffaut's film she exudes charm and confidence as the appealing, seductive Fabienne. Although she doesn't have the biggest part in *Stolen Kisses*—and despite what she may have thought—Seyrig steals every single scene she appears in. This is highly representative of Seyrig's entire career, as every time she was cast in a non-starring role she ended up quietly walking away with the film, even if that was never her intention. There is perhaps no better example of this than in Jacques Demy's live-action fairytale *Once Upon a Time/Donkey Skin* (*Peau d'âne*, 1970), in which Seyrig's supporting turn distracts from lead actress Catherine Deneuve, a performer who counts as one of *the* great movie stars. It was very difficult to hide Seyrig in a film and her numerous cameo roles, by virtue of their obtrusiveness, more or less prove her star quality. Delphine Seyrig was no character actor, and her

Delphine Seyrig in 1969.

presence in a movie was such that to ration it seemed to be cheating the audience, who not unreasonably wanted to see stars starring in movies.

While *Last Year at Marienbad* proved to be Seyrig's big break, her character—like all others in the film—was little more than a cipher in a *mise-en-scène* in which the aesthetic of Alains Resnais and Robbe-

Grillet was king; it is rather telling that the film's characters aren't assigned names, but are denoted by single letters. Seyrig crashed into the public eye with *Marienbad*, but it would be wrong to assume that she'd simply, suddenly, walked into a starring role in a major film:

> She looks like she was born there in *Marienbad*. However, she has ten years of theater behind her, ten years of touring in the provinces, a succession of failures and successes without tomorrow, galleries in New York, where she attended the courses of [Lee] Strasberg and played in a film of the Beat Generation [short *Pull My Daisy*, 1959]. Resnais saved her from despair, anxiety and tears, but he also erased those years. He offered her the proposal she dreamed of, a sumptuous and magical film which will make her leave anonymity behind. (Brangé, 2018: 14–15)

Muriel was Delphine Seyrig's second and last feature film with Alain Resnais; while beginning work on the film, both parties were riding high on the great success of *Marienbad*, yet it soon became clear that its follow-up would present some significant logistical challenges. The key decisions to film in color and greatly extend the running time (from eighty minutes to nearly two hours) meant that *Muriel*'s painstakingly-obtained budget was soon exceeded (ibid.: 196). Compared to the glamorous, Chanel-clad character Seyrig essayed in *Marienbad*, *Muriel*'s Hélène was quite a departure, at least in terms of appearance. Hélène, the widow with the adult stepson, certainly *seems* much older than *Marienbad*'s A, yet it is hard to determine—even approximately—how old she is without the help of Jean Cayrol's script, which informs us that Hélène is thirty-eight but "could pass for a slightly-damaged twenty years, or […] [a] forty-five years on which fatigue and worries have put their claws" (1963: 17). This is a near-perfect description of Hélène as played by Seyrig, who was thirty when she starred in *Muriel* yet, within a tolerance of roughly a dozen years, could seemingly age or de-age at will. Curiously, Cayrol describes Hélène as being at "the frailest age of a woman", presumably because middle age is just around the corner (ibid.: 33). In *Muriel*, Seyrig exhibited what was to become her trademark manner, which might be summed up as warm yet inscrutable. The attentions of Alphonse and Roland make it clear that Hélène is considered to be an attractive woman, albeit one "of a certain age" (for want of a better expression), and the relative deglamorizing of Seyrig did little to diminish neither her natural beauty nor her star quality. In her review for *Film Quarterly*, Susan Sontag noted how:

> *Muriel* is dominated by a single performance. The performance of the ravishing Delphine Seyrig as Hélène is, in the peculiarly cinematic sense of the word, that of a star. Mlle. Seyrig has the nourishing irrelevant panoply of mannerisms of a star; that is to say, she doesn't simply play (or even perfectly fill) a role. She becomes an independent aesthetic object in herself. Each detail of her appearance—her greying hair, her tilted loping walk, her wide-brimmed hats and smartly dowdy suits, her gauche manner in enthusiasm and regret—is indelible, unnecessary, delightful. (1964)

Delphine Seyrig as Hélène in *Muriel*.

Muriel was undoubtedly the film in which Delphine Seyrig made the transition to bona fide star, and Sontag goes on to make the point that "Seyrig wasn't a star in *L'Année dernière à Marienbad* [...] [b]ut she is, in *Muriel*. In *Muriel*, she joins that small company of genuine star presences ([Jean-Paul] Belmondo, Jeanne Moreau, Jean-Pierre Cassell, Annie Girardot)" (ibid.). Almost twenty years on from Sontag's review, Vincent Canby drew comparison with one of the all-time greats, commenting that Seyrig possessed "a screen presence comparable, perhaps, only to Garbo" (1983). It is both surprising and slightly unfortunate that *Muriel* marked the end of Seyrig's work with Resnais, although it may have been a wise move on the part of both: *Muriel*, unlike *Marienbad*, could not be topped, so it would have been foolish to try. Neither its star nor its director made a better film in their careers, and their parting of ways after the exhausting, exacting *Muriel* could be interpreted as both parties considering the film to be an apex of sorts.

The distracted, slightly flaky Hélène was far removed from the actress who played her, who was both whip-smart and politically engaged. Seyrig had her own ideas as to why *Muriel*'s difficult subject matter had largely been avoided by filmmakers, explaining how "[t]he Algerian War was painfully felt and cineastes don't talk about it; they say that they will not get past censorship roadblocks. Resnais thinks that it's rather a self-censorship, a real problem in filming the war in Algeria", and further noting how Resnais tried to tackle the subject in a novel way via Jean Cayrol's script (Buache, 1987: 6). This notion of censorship, both internal and external, had been raised several years before the filming of *Muriel*:

> The CNC [France's National Center for Cinema and the Moving Image], which had refused authorization to shoot films that touched on contemporary politics in general, was implacable regarding the Algerian war in particular. As Jacques Doniol-Valcroze wrote in *France-Observateur*, "On the political scene, French censorship is *very* severe. We hardly notice it because, this state of mind being known, there is a preliminary auto-censorship and almost all French films are devoid of political audacity". *Le Petit*

Soldat would be the first film by a recognized producer to deal explicitly with the war in Algeria. Godard complained that "young directors, those less than forty years old, have the idea of censorship in their heads the moment that they make a film"; he said that "they shouldn't worry about it," and set out to show why not. (Brody, 2008)

The cementing of Seyrig's star status with *Muriel*—for which she won Best Actress at the 1963 Venice Film Festival—meant that she was always going to be in demand from then on. In some ways, she could be described as a director's actor, and her presence in a film guaranteed a certain level of quality, albeit one that didn't always equate with commercial success. In her book *Stars and Stardom in French Cinema*, Ginette Vincendeau includes Seyrig in a group of "actresses with minimal box-office power but a strong auteur filmography" (2000: 28). *Hiroshima mon amour* writer Marguerite Duras, who directed Delphine Seyrig in several films including the well-received *India Song* (1975), memorably referred to Seyrig as an "unknown celebrity" (Brangé, 2018: 15). In addition to those filmmakers already mentioned, Seyrig worked with other notable directors including Luis Buñuel, Joseph Losey, Don Siegel, Harry Kümel and Fred Zinnemann. Seyrig was perfectly fluent in English, which naturally increased her choice of roles, and she remains best known to non-Francophone audiences for her role in Zinnemann's *The Day of the Jackal* (1973), which will be discussed in chapter 5.

As a strong advocate of women's rights, Seyrig frequently used her celebrity status to further feminist goals. Throughout much of her career, she demonstrated a predilection for those female directors, such the aforementioned Varda and Duras, who had established themselves in what was, and remains, a male-dominated vocation. Seyrig also appeared in films by directors Liliane de Kermadec (who had served as *Muriel*'s stills photographer), Ulrike Ottinger, and Chantal Akerman, working with each on more than one occasion.

It is with the last of these, the great Belgian director Akerman, that Seyrig formed a particularly formidable partnership, and the pair collaborated on the visually austere *Jeanne Dielman, 23 quai du Commerce, 1080 Bruxelles* (1975). This formally rigorous movie, which at a little over two hundred minutes boasts a running time as unwieldy as its title, stands as one of Seyrig's career highlights and is a prime example of the actress' conscious pulling away from the glamorous movie star image she had cultivated in *Marienbad*. Whether she ever completed this process, which had begun as early as *Muriel*, is debatable, and one reviewer of *Jeanne Dielman* gushed that the film's star had "never looked more beautiful" (Canby, 1983). Despite her efforts to shake off the legacy of her feature debut, *Marienbad*'s shadow was always present, and Mireille Brangé draws an interesting comparison, noting how Seyrig, "unlike her character in the film, [...] would never escape completely from the labyrinth" (2018: 15). As if to underline this point, Brangé's excellent, detailed biography of Seyrig uses an iconic shot of the actress in *Last Year at Marienbad* as its front cover illustration. The plumed Chanel cape worn by Seyrig in *Marienbad* may have been responsible for an image which instantly seared itself into the collective memory of arthouse cinema, but it also reduced its wearer to something of a mannequin.

As has already been established, the short journey from one Alain Resnais film to another saw Seyrig lurch from a position where she served the material to one where she dominated the show. While *Muriel* does contain some stylized elements, it is a very different work from *Marienbad*—a film that could be said to have plenty of ice but perhaps not enough fire. Just as in *Marienbad*, *Muriel* saw Seyrig play an amnesiac, but the role of Hélène allowed the actress much more room in which to exhibit her considerable range. Although *Muriel* is as synonymous with Delphine Seyrig as it is with Boulogne, the actress doesn't take over the film in some obvious, showy, scenery-chewing manner, but instead draws the viewer's attention with her subtly magnetic presence. Given Seyrig's status as the face of the film, it's very easy, even after countless viewings, to lazily refer to Seyrig's Hélène as Muriel; such a pitfall wasn't really possible with *Marienbad*. In *Last Year at Marienbad*, Seyrig *looked* every inch the movie star, but it took until *Muriel* for this status to be confirmed.

Anyone who remembers the first time they saw Alfred Hitchcock's *Psycho* (1960) will likely remember the spectacular way in which the film pulls the rug from under the audience's feet. In its early stages, *Psycho* sets itself up as the story of Marion Crane, a woman who embezzles a large sum of money before heading cross country to meet up with her debt-ridden boyfriend. During her road trip, Marion arouses the suspicions of the police, and it looks as if we're set for further twists in this pulpy tale of a good girl gone bad and her efforts to outwit the law. Except, at around the forty-five-minute mark, Marion stops at a motel where she is stabbed to death, and the establishment's proprietor promptly takes over as *Psycho*'s main character. *Psycho*'s immense popularity over the past six decades has seen the film reduced to a synecdoche of a cross-dressing knife-wielding maniac, and it's easy to forget that the film starts off as something approximating a rote, if admittedly thrilling, crime drama.

Hitch, who was François Truffaut's idol and eventually cast Claude Jade (the female lead in Truffaut's Antoine Doinel films) in *Topaz* (1969), makes a brief appearance in *Muriel* (well, a life-sized cutout of him does), and Resnais' film bears a resemblance to *Psycho* insofar as it is also a work in which one main character is eventually supplanted by another. In *Muriel*, this process is far more subtle than it is in *Psycho*, in which false protagonist Marion is quite literally chopped out of the movie, and the elliptical nature of *Muriel* means that this development is much harder to identify. Yet as *Muriel* progresses, Bernard surreptitiously moves to the forefront of the film, and by the movie's end Hélène has firmly taken a back seat as her troubled stepson's story plays out. Given *Muriel*'s unusual structure, Bernard's gradual takeover is easy to miss, and it doesn't jump out at the viewer in anything like the same manner as Marion's death in *Psycho*, which could be likened to the moment in *L.A. Confidential* (1997) in which the film killed off what, to that point, had appeared to be its main character. *Muriel* can be viewed as a triptych, of sorts: it begins with Hélène's story, which is then eclipsed by the tragedy of the absent Muriel, which in turn feeds into the unraveling of Bernard. Interestingly, Resnais saw his film as more of an ensemble piece, stating that "the title does not imply for us that Muriel, therefore the story of Bernard, is the real center of the film. For us, all of the characters in the film are 'central'" (Bounoure, 1962).

Although Jean-Baptiste Thiérrée's Bernard may eventually end up as *Muriel*'s central character, this does little to distract from Seyrig's presence; *Muriel* is always Delphine Seyrig's show, and it is testament to her generosity as a performer that she can give way to a younger performer like Thiérrée, even if all eyes remain on her. Marion Crane and Jack Vincennes are soon forgotten in *Psycho* and *L.A. Confidential* respectively, and although Hélène has a distinct advantage over those two in that she doesn't exit the film, her shift further back is barely noticed due to Seyrig's singular screen presence. In her monograph on Harry Kümel's Seyrig-starring vampire movie *Daughters of Darkness* (*Les lèvres rouges*, 1971), Kat Ellinger commented that "there was no-one quite like her, and nor is it likely there ever will be" (2020: 15). It is often tempting to think that the concepts of the movie star and the great actor are mutually exclusive but, both in and after *Muriel*, Delphine Seyrig proved that it is perfectly possible to be both.

Jackal, Soldier, Antique Dealer: *Muriel*, Malraux, and the OAS

Chapter Five

THE FRENCH SEAPORT of Le Havre, like Boulogne, was rebuilt from the ground up following the Second World War; in a further link to *Muriel*, the city is also the hometown of Jean-Pierre Kérien, the actor who played the nefarious Alphonse Noyard. Havre boasts a particularly striking building known as *Le Volcan* (The Volcano), which was designed by famed Brazilian architect Oscar Niemeyer. *Le Volcan* was once the home of France's very first *maison de la culture* (literally, "culture house"), which opened in 1961 at what is now the excellent André Malraux Museum of Modern Art, before moving on to the *Volcan* via the Théâtre de l'Hôtel Ville. The *maison*'s first site was where Jacques Rivette's sprawling, thirteen-hour *Out 1: Noli Me Tangere* (1971) enjoyed its first public screening, and this legendary film plays like a Who's Who of great French actors of the era: Juliet Berto, Jean-Pierre Léaud, Bernadette Lafont, Bulle Ogier, Michèle Moretti, Françoise Fabian—plus that distinguished Franco–British performer Michael Lonsdale, who acted alongside Delphine Seyrig on many occasions.

It's fitting that the museum now carries the name of the man who, in launching the *maison de la culture* initiative, enabled many French citizens' constitutional "right to culture" by decentralizing the French arts scene, which had previously been very Paris-centric. In 1959, just as the Algerian War was coming to the boil, André Malraux was appointed France's first Minister of Cultural Affairs by Charles de

Gaulle, and he went on to hold this post for over a decade. In 1962 both Malraux and de Gaulle survived assassination attempts, and the attempt on Malraux's life, while unsuccessful, had particularly terrible consequences; this, and André Malraux's links to *Muriel*, will be discussed presently.

The attacks on Malraux and de Gaulle were carried out by the *Organisation Armée Secrète* (Secret Army Organization, or OAS), a right-wing operation vehemently opposed to Algerian independence. The OAS was formed in Francoist Spain in early 1961, adopting the motto *L'Algérie est française et le restera* (Algeria is French and will remain so). The movement, which was mainly made up of a number of cells based in both Algeria and mainland France, viewed itself as a counter-terrorist organization and considered its work to be on a par with that of the French Resistance in WWII. If we broadly assume the two opposing sides of the Algerian War to be France and the FLN, the OAS presented a further complication in that they considered both de Gaulle's government and the FLN to be their enemies, and consequently went to war against both belligerents:

> [On September 8, 1961], de Gaulle narrowly escaped being blown up by the OAS at Pont-sur-Seine. The fact that this was carried out by an autonomous cell, operating on the mainland under a dissident officer, Lieutenant-Colonel Bastien Thierry, emphasized the lack of overall control. The acronym OAS was the facade for many different groups which [...] carried out bombings and assassinations on their own initiative. Beginning on 31 May 1961, when one cell stabbed to death a senior police officer [...] in central Algiers, these groups unleashed a spiral of bloodshed during the summer and autumn. Some of this violence was aimed at specific targets—FLN opposite numbers, policemen, communists, 'third force' moderates—but some were indiscriminate killing as OAS operatives, circulating anonymously in cars and on scooters, machine-gunned Algerian cafés or seized upon Algerian passers-by on the grounds that 'any dead Arab will do'. (Evans, 2012)

The formation of the OAS effectively turned the conflict into a triangular war, and the last thing the organization wanted was for the established opposing sides to enter into talks with one another, yet that is exactly what transpired. Once a ceasefire had been negotiated between the FLN and Paris, the OAS carried out a sustained bombing campaign, detonating over one hundred bombs a day—against targets including hospitals and schools—in the hope that it would force the FLN to abandon the armistice. As the OAS' activities eventually stretched to mainland France, the French public realized that the war had become far messier and couldn't be ring-fenced within the overseas territory. While *Muriel* doesn't go as far as to name the organization, it is almost certain that Robert both belongs to the movement and is behind the bombing of Bernard's workroom. In Jean Cayrol's script, it is Bernard himself who is described as "ticking like a bomb", yet his figurative explosion occurs just before the literal one that destroys his sanctuary (1963: 21). Charles de Gaulle survived a number of assassination attempts, but the OAS attack in 1961 in which a plastic bomb (much like the one in *Muriel*) failed to detonate was one of two which came very close to killing the president; the other, the aforementioned 1962 effort, was detailed in Fred Zinnemann's *The Day of the Jackal*.

Zinnemann's filmography, which makes for impressive reading, includes *The Search* (1948), *Julia* (1977), *High Noon* (1952), *A Man for All Seasons* (1966), *The Sundowners* (1960), *Oklahoma!* (1955) and, what is perhaps his best-known movie, *From Here to Eternity* (1953). Films directed by Zinnemann garnered a total of two dozen Academy Awards, and he came to *The Day of the Jackal*, which was to be his third-last film, fresh from winning the best director Oscar for *A Man for All Seasons*. So it is reasonable to say that great things were expected of Zinnemann's adaptation of Frederick Forsyth's bestselling novel of the same name, to which the filming rights had been snapped up shortly after the book was first published in 1971; thankfully, the resulting film didn't disappoint.

The Day of the Jackal is a film in which the OAS plays a large, critical part, given that this lengthy (yet wire-tight) thriller centers on the organization's attempts to kill President de Gaulle. While, as has already been mentioned, de Gaulle was no stranger to efforts to assassinate him, Zinnemann's film, like the source novel it closely follows, blurs the lines between fact and fiction in having the story begin with the 1962 incident, wherein the unarmored Citroën DS limousine in which de Gaulle and his wife were traveling came under heavy machine-gun fire. This recreation of a real-life occurrence is shown in the first few minutes of the film, but once this is dispensed with the story takes a sharp-left turn into a fictional scenario in which Edward Fox's mysterious, debonair Jackal is hired by the OAS. Given the resounding failure of the organization to eliminate the president, the Jackal has been tasked with assassinating de Gaulle, and we proceed to watch the Jackal and his extensive collection of ascots clandestinely make their way around a France in which no-one appears to speak French. In an absorbing climax, the Jackal finally gets the president in his crosshairs only to be foiled by the police, who have been led to the scene by Michael Lonsdale's dogged and sleep-deprived Deputy Commissioner Lebel.

Although *The Day of the Jackal* ends with a thwarted assassination attempt—and there were plenty of those during de Gaulle's presidency—this particular effort never actually happened, so in this respect the movie bears heavy similarities to *Muriel*; both films present us with fictionalized events (the torture and murder of Muriel, the Jackal's attempt on de Gaulle's life), yet we know that these closely relate to real-life occurrences. This muddying of the waters makes these films' contents far more upsetting and disturbing than any work of pure fiction, as the audience is painfully aware that the smallest of margins separates these acts from their factual counterparts. The two films share a connection beyond their depictions of the OAS in that both occur within the same timeline, and the fortnight in which *Muriel* unfolds fits comfortably inside the year and three days in which *The Day of the Jackal* occurs, meaning that as Hélène is carefully preparing dinner, the Jackal is meticulously planning his attack on the president. Additionally, both films feature actors Delphine Seyrig and Jean Champion (*Muriel*'s Ernest), who in Zinnemann's film respectively play Baroness Colette de Montpellier and a detective. Although, as already noted, the film is a faithful adaptation of the novel, Seyrig's character sports a different surname from the one given in the novel (in which she's known as Colette de la Chalonniere). While, in film as in book, both Colettes are aristocratic types who are seduced and subsequently murdered by the title character, Forsyth's novel gives the character a backstory, one which is absent from the film yet better explains the Baroness' actions:

> She looked back at the cutting from the Paris glossy society magazine that her friend had so thoughtfully mailed to her; at the face of her husband grinning inanely into the flash-bulb, eyes torn between the lens of the camera and the jutting bosom of the starlet over whose shoulder he was peering. A cabaret dancer, risen from bar hostess, quoted as saying she hoped 'one day' to be able to marry the Baron, who was her 'very good friend'. Looking at the lined face and scrawny neck of the ageing Baron in the photograph, she wondered vaguely what had happened to the handsome young captain of the Resistance partisans with whom she had fallen in love in 1942 and married a year later when she was expecting her son. She had been a teenage girl, running messages for the Resistance, when she met him in the mountains […]. Then after the war had come the restoration of all his lands and properties […]. Soon the estates had tired him, the lure of Paris and the lights of the cabarets, the urge to make up for the lost years of his manhood in the undergrowth had proved too strong to resist. Now he was fifty-seven and could have passed for seventy. (1971: 335–336)

Seyrig's presence in *The Day of the Jackal* provides yet another example of the way in which the actress frequently became the defining memory of the films she appeared in—including those in which she didn't play the main character. Although Seyrig's turn in the film is predictably memorable, there is a sense that her character has had her story arc truncated, and study of the novel appears to confirm this. That said, there's an economy to the character as seen in the film, and to include the sort of exposition as quoted above would have stripped Colette of the inscrutable air that Seyrig channels so effortlessly. The omission of Colette's backstory may simply have been due to constraints of length; even as it stands, *The Day of the Jackal* is a busy film that comes close to the two-and-a-half-hour mark. Another reason for the apparent streamlining of the character on the screen lies in the film's apparent desire to operate within the tolerance of its PG limits, and a franker depiction of the liaisons between Colette and the Jackal as per the book would have seen the film slapped with a higher rating.

The Day of the Jackal is probably as hard a PG as there is but, as the scenes involving Colette prove, Fred Zinnemann was clearly keen to avoid anything too explicit. However, the scaling back of the book's sexual content pales in comparison to the way in which the film dilutes Forsyth's representation of torture. While the film presents us with a torture scene which is admittedly at the upper limits of family-friendly viewing, the corresponding section in Forsyth's book is a brutal and explicit passage, one which recalls the real-life ordeal of Henri Alleg in *La Question*:

> If we have to we keep you alive and conscious for days, weeks. No merciful oblivion like in the old days. One is technical nowadays. There are drugs, *tu sais* [you know]. Third degree is finished now, probably gone for good. So why not talk. [...] Lolling against the chest, the great head shook slowly from side to side. It was as if the closed eyes were examining first one and then the other of the little copper crabs that gripped the nipples, or the single larger one whose serrated teeth clipped each side of the head of the penis. [...] The electric switch went on. The little metal crabs fixed to the man in the chair [...] appeared to come alive with a slight buzzing. In silence the huge form in the chair rose as if by levitation, propelled by an unseen hand in the small of the back. The legs and wrists bulged outwards against the straps until it seemed that even with the padding the leather must cut clean through the flesh and bone. The eyes, medically unable to see clearly through the puffed flesh around them, defied medicine and started outwards bulging into vision and staring at the ceiling above. The mouth was open as if in surprise and it was half a second before the demonic scream came out of the lungs. When it did come, it went on and on and on. (1971: 173–174)

As a marker of just how messy the Algerian War had become, *The Day of the Jackal* offers yet another permutation of the torturers and the tortured, with France now seen to be brutalizing an OAS member (it's an OAS bodyguard who's on the receiving end of the treatment outlined in the above quote).

Chacal (to change it up for a moment and give this British–French production its alternative title) features a couple of other performers mentioned elsewhere in this book, including Olga Georges-Picot, who plays the OAS mole Denise; previously, Georges-Picot was the striking female lead in *Je t'aime, je t'aime* (1968), Alain Resnais' next film but one after *Muriel*, which will be discussed in detail in chapter 6. Denise is a sizable role, and the character plays a key part in *The Day of the Jackal*'s twisty plot. However, an actor who has a greater thematic connection with the topic of Zinnemann's film is *Le petit soldat*'s star Michel Subor, who has a brief, uncredited role as an OAS member. Despite the brevity of his appearance, Subor is easy to spot, and one can't help but wonder if his casting is a nod to his defining role in Jean-Luc Godard's film; otherwise, he's an actor who seems way too big for his part, and he'd already made himself known to international audiences through his substantial role in Hitchcock's *Topaz*, in which he played the husband of Delphine Seyrig's *Stolen Kisses* co-star Claude Jade (who, just like Seyrig, would die of cancer aged just fifty-eight). *Topaz*, like *The Day of the Jackal*, was another thriller that had been fast-tracked from bestselling novel to film in the space of a couple of years; *The Day of the Jackal*'s producer and screenwriter would move quickly to bring another Frederick Forsyth book to the screen in the same short timeframe with *The Odessa File* (1974).

While Subor, like the Algerian War, provides a link between *Le petit soldat* and *The Day of the Jackal*, his role in the latter unfortunately serves to further misguide those who are still under the impression that his Forestier in *Le petit soldat* works for the OAS; there is a staggering amount of writing out there that incorrectly refers to Forestier as an OAS operative. As noted in chapter 3, Forestier was more than likely working for the Red Hand, an outfit operated by France's External Documentation and Counter-Espionage Service (SDECE); when Godard made *Le petit soldat*, the OAS had yet to be formed (Lack, 2003). By the time *Le petit soldat* was released, the organization was largely defunct, yet it had achieved wide notoriety for its terror campaign during the Algerian conflict, so perhaps this partly explains the willingness of many to retcon Forestier into the OAS. However, the assumption that the OAS has any sort of bearing on *Le petit soldat* doesn't help anyone when it comes to disentangling screen representations of an already confusing war.

While *The Day of the Jackal* centered on the OAS' quest to assassinate de Gaulle, there's never been a film devoted to the organization's attempt on André Malraux's life. Yet Malraux, through both his ministerial position and his daughter Florence's work as an assistant director (AD), had concrete links to cinema in general, while *Muriel* was of particular relevance to the statesman, given that it featured a plotline involving the OAS and was directed by his son-in-law-to-be. Florence was an AD on *Muriel*, and performed this same role on nine of her husband's other features spanning a quarter of a century from *Last Year at Marienbad* to *Mélo* (1986); she's also prominently credited as the "Executive Mentor" of *I Want to Go Home* (1989).

André Malraux had already made his name as a successful novelist before the Second World War—a copy of one of his books is briefly glimpsed in *Le petit soldat*—and during the conflict he distinguished himself through serving with the French Army then the Resistance, receiving several medals for his contributions to the war against the Nazis (he'd previously fought against fascism during the Spanish Civil War). In the postwar years, Malraux made for a valuable appointment to de Gaulle's government, given his own direct experiences of the French arts scene. Yet it was this role that nearly cost Malraux his life: while the OAS was continually chasing the top prize in the form of de Gaulle, it also looked to claim the life of any then-incumbent government minister. As someone who had achieved success in multiple areas—the arts, the military, politics, and so on—to the extent where he easily qualified for the title of polymath, Malraux represented a high-profile target for the OAS as it waged its campaign on the French mainland.

The bombing of the absent Malraux's home in Paris' leafy western suburbs may have failed in its attempt to kill the minister, but the explosion blinded four-year-old Delphine Renard in another apartment. The OAS, in a move which highlighted the organization at its most amateur, had failed to identify that Malraux rented the

André Malraux in 1974.

building's two upper floors, and the plastic bomb was planted on a ground floor windowsill which belonged to the little girl's bedroom (Renard, 2013). As the device detonated, the window's shattered glass caused dreadful injuries, and doctors only just managed to save the young girl's life; Delphine credits her great love of reading as a major factor in her survival, recalling how she was both lying on the ground and immersed in a book when the bomb went off (ibid.). The child's bloodied, disfigured face appeared on the cover of French weekly magazine *Paris Match*, accompanied by a caption reading *ce visage mutilé accuse l'OAS* (this mutilated face accuses the OAS); if the publication ever lived down to delivering *le choc des photos* (the shock of photos) its motto threatened, then surely this was that moment (ibid.).

Those still laboring under the misapprehension that the OAS consisted of freedom fighters serving a noble cause were given a sharp wake-up call by this terrible image. It didn't take long for Jean-Marie Vincent, an important figure in the OAS' Parisian network, to be apprehended and charged with attempted murder (Madsen, 2015). Happily, Delphine Renard went on to forge a career as an eminent psychoanalyst, a profession she still practices to this day, and in her excellent autobiography she recalls a pleasant surprise meeting with *Muriel*'s director:

> Venice, 1977. I walk down the street with my mother, discovering churches and paintings. A smiling couple walks forward to meet us. "It's Florence Malraux and Alain Resnais," my mother whispered to me before reaching out to them. The coincidences are imperfect: I should have met Florence in Florence, a city so loved by her mother Clara. (2013)

A terrible irony of the attack that maimed Delphine was that André Malraux had always appeared to be somewhat ambivalent toward de Gaulle's decision to grant independence to Algeria, and there were other high-profile politicians whose support for the move clearly exceeded that of the Culture Minister. It is hard to know how the assassination attempt informed *Muriel*, but given André Malraux's close personal connection to two of the filmmakers, it is hard to imagine that the bombing didn't figure in Alain Resnais' thinking as he prepared to film his take on the Algerian conflict. *Muriel*'s refusal to name the OAS could be interpreted as an unwillingness to give the organization any more recognition, or it might be viewed as an avoidance of provocation, given the Malraux family's close shave with the OAS.

Prior to both *Muriel* and the assassination attempt, the relationship between André Malraux and his daughter had survived a potentially awkward moment in 1960, when Florence signed what has since become known as the "Manifesto of the 121". This document was an open letter to the French government (which of course included André Malraux), requesting both an end to the French Army's use of torture and recognition of the Algerian conflict as a legitimate struggle for independence. The petition was formed of an illustrious list of names; beyond Florence Malraux and Alain Resnais, signatories included Truffaut, Sartre, de Beauvoir, Robbe-Grillet and Duras. Shortly after the list's publication (in magazine *Vérité-Liberté*), more names were added, including writer Clara Malraux (André's ex-wife and Florence's mother), *Cahiers* editor Jacques Doniol-Valcroze, and *Muriel* producer Anatole Dauman. One name, however, was conspicuous by its absence, as Jean-Luc Godard had swerved the document, seeing as "[h]e still hoped to have a *visa de contrôle* [distribution certificate; emphasis added] for *Le Petit Soldat*, and on top of that, he was a foreigner" (Brody, 2008). The government's crackdown on those who signed was both immediate and severe, with all signatories "banned from television and radio appearances, state-subsidized theaters, and government-aided films—which meant, for all practical purposes, all films" (ibid.). Alain Resnais aired his feelings on such censorship:

> We are threatened with real Spanish-style censorship, since, according to a recent decree, all scenarios must be approved by a commission. Reasons regarding morality are given, but I don't believe that much. Moreover, until now, censorship has always been extremely lenient in terms of morality. The powers of the current commission would have been more than sufficient to curb the possible

deviations of the filmmakers. And if we wanted to change the formula, it was to institute political intolerance. The maneuver is to use the pretext of a "license" that has been allowed to take hold to strengthen censorship in general. What threatens us is "moral order" in all its forms. The problem would however be simple to solve: apart from the prohibition of certain films to minors, it would suffice to specify, as for the press, which ideas or which feelings (racial hatred, certain types of violence, etc.) it is forbidden to disseminate. But what they want to introduce is arbitrary. (Bounoure, 1962)

However, given everything else that was going on at the time, the government eventually backed off at the very real prospect of a French spin on McCarthyism. Although it may quite reasonably be assumed that the ill feeling between the government and those who signed the petition made for some uneasy parent–child moments within the Malraux family, André and Florence were on the same page in condemning the French Army's use of torture, and Malraux Sr. had some innovative ideas as to how the conflict might be resolved, at least temporarily:

[In Algeria], we spruce up what's Arabic and Muslim to the point where even in Egypt people will talk about this model zone as a Mecca. We must make Algerians proud of cooperating with France and make all other Arabs [...] jealous of the people living in this zone. This doesn't mean we shouldn't negotiate and it doesn't cancel political decisions, but it creates a mystique of accomplishments, the only weapon that we have against the "allure" of the *Front de liberation national* [...]. Later we can then build a Franco-North African federation because for a change the peoples of North Africa will have seen the advantage of cooperating with us. At the same time, we can rebuild France by giving ourselves a goal. (Madsen, 2015)

While André Malraux may have met with immense professional success, he also suffered some terrible personal tragedies. After separating from Clara, Malraux entered into a relationship with the journalist Josette Clotis, and the couple had two sons, Vincent and Gauthier. The boys were only babies when, with WWII nearing its conclusion, their mother slipped while alighting a moving train and was crushed between two carriages. Josette died a few hours after the accident, aged just thirty-four. Worse was to come for Malraux in May 1961, when the Alfa Romeo driven by Gauthier skidded off a slippery road west of Dijon and crashed into a tree, killing both the driver and Vincent, who was in the passenger seat (ibid.). Most of us will hopefully never have to endure the immense grief Malraux would have experienced; the two boys and their mother, whose cumulative age totaled less than the seventy-five years André Malraux would live to, share a grave in Paris' Charonne Cemetery. Less than nine months on from the untimely deaths of Vincent and Gauthier, the OAS would bomb the grieving Malraux's apartment building. Shortly after the attack of February 1962, André Malraux moved out of the apartment and Delphine Renard, who shared Josette's birthday of April 8, moved into the bedroom once occupied by Vincent and Gauthier, whose tenancy was rather poignantly marked by an indelible ink stain on the parquet floor (Renard, 2013).

Malraux, who died in 1976, achieved a great deal in his time on this earth, and in 2011 his name was one of those mentioned in historian Arthur M. Schlesinger Jr.'s swathe of interviews with First Lady Jacqueline Kennedy. These interviews were conducted in early 1964, just a few months after President Kennedy's death, but the transcripts weren't made publicly available until almost half a century had elapsed. In the book, Jackie Kennedy—both a Francophile and a Francophone—refers to Malraux, whom she'd made a special request to meet, as "the most fascinating man I've ever talked to", which is high praise indeed considering the barbs aimed at others including Malraux's boss de Gaulle ("spiteful"), Martin Luther King ("terrible"), and Indira Gandhi ("horrible"), but possibly not what the late JFK would have wanted to hear (Kennedy and Beschloss, 2011). The Kennedys first met Malraux during a 1961 state visit to France, which occurred just a few days after the deaths of Gauthier and Vincent. Despite this double tragedy, André Malraux continued with his ministerial duties, and Jackie Kennedy recalled Malraux's entrance at the first night reception at the Élysée Palace, describing his face as:

> all white and puffy from crying through the receiving— and all Malraux's tics going at once. And the whole place just fell into a hush. But obviously, it [meeting Malraux] was the one thing I'd asked [for] and so it was—So the next day, Malraux took me to the Jeu de Paume [museum] and then after, [the Château de] Malmaison, and then he was fine. And I think it gave him, in a way—I don't know, I suppose it's good to have something to do after something like that happens. But that's when our friendship started. (ibid.)

Two-and-a-half years after the Kennedys first meeting with Malraux, President Kennedy met his end in Dallas (on the day when the fictional *The Odessa File* commences). JFK could well have used some of the luck de Gaulle and Malraux experienced when faced with the various attempts on their lives, but Jack Kennedy's death meant that Malraux, a man who had prematurely lost three of his nearest and dearest in tragic circumstances, suddenly had something in common with Jackie Kennedy that neither would have wished for. There is a curious link between the fate of Jack Kennedy and the one intended for both de Gaulle and Malraux in the form of New Orleans businessman Clay Shaw, the only person to be tried in connection with JFK's assassination. Shaw, who was decorated by both the US and France for his service in WWII, was acquitted of the charges, but some believed that he had links to the OAS, and this is mentioned in Oliver Stone's *JFK* (1991), which also references the 1962 attempt on de Gaulle's life that was featured in *The Day of the Jackal*. Had this attempt on de Gaulle's life succeeded, the presidents of two major Western powers would have been assassinated in the space of little over a year, and for Shaw, who sat on the board of shadowy holding company Permindex, to be associated with both attacks was extremely damaging to his reputation, despite the lack of any convictions. Shaw died just five years after his acquittal.

Although it was the First Lady who instigated the meeting with Malraux, which says much about the latter's stature and reputation, it seems that the road went both ways and Jackie O left a lasting impression on the revered author and statesman, who dedicated his autobiography *Anti-Memoirs* to "Mrs. John Fitzgerald Kennedy" (1968). It is slightly unfortunate that this Renaissance man is not better known outside of the French-speaking world, as history has shown André Malraux to be one of the great minds of the twentieth century. Upon Malraux's death, President Valéry Giscard-d'Estaing, in a message to Florence, praised her father's life as one defined by an "exceptional dialogue between creative work and action" (Madsen, 2015).

Another film in which the OAS features heavily is Alain Cavalier's *The Unvanquished/Have I the Right to Kill?* (*L'Insoumis*, 1964), in which Alain Delon plays Thomas, a Luxembourgish divorcé who joins the French Foreign Legion, only to desert after he's posted to Algeria during the war. Thomas is enticed into joining the OAS by his former lieutenant, and is soon involved in the kidnapping of Lea Massari's Dominique, a French lawyer who has flown into Algiers to defend two Algerian nationalists. The captured Dominique is locked in the bathroom of an apartment, but Thomas secretly helps the prisoner by supplying her with much-needed drinks via a straw through the keyhole. Thomas decides to free Dominique, but is caught by one of his colleagues; during the ensuing firefight, Thomas sustains a serious gunshot wound but escapes with the lawyer.

Dominique returns home safely, and Thomas is smuggled out of Algeria on a boat bound for mainland France, whereupon he takes a train to Luxembourg. Before the train gets to Thomas' destination, he alights and heads to see Dominique at her home. Dominique tends to Thomas' injury, and a romance blossoms between the two, but the OAS tracks them down. Thomas again manages to shoot his way out of the predicament, and he and Dominique flee in the lawyer's car. Roadblocks make the couple's journey extremely hazardous, but eventually the severely ailing Thomas gets out of the car and crosses the border alone on foot. He makes it to his mother's house, only to die from his injuries shortly after.

The Unvanquished was something of a personal project for Alain Delon who, as with the previous year's *Any Number Can Win*, produced the film through his own company. At that point in his career, Delon was a major box-office star, one thought of as a sure thing when it came to opening a movie. To the surprise of many, not least its producer-star, *The Unvanquished* was not a success on its initial release, and its commercial failure effectively marked the moment when the French

Alain Delon in 1959.

public signaled that it had endured sufficient reminders about the dispiriting mess that was the Algerian War. While the film's lackluster performance didn't threaten the deal Delon had with MGM, for which *The Unvanquished* was the third of five pictures, its cool reception proved that not even Delon could make this material enticing to mainstream audiences. Unlike the other OAS-related films mentioned in this chapter, *The Unvanquished* required cuts to be made before it was considered suitable for theatrical release; the unexpurgated version, which is now presumably lost forever, would have made for intriguing viewing.

The Unvanquished is never less than an engrossing film, but it's also a strangely tame, muted one, and in many ways it plays like a movie from a much earlier time. Part of this may be attributed to its censorial travails, but there is no doubt that Claude Renoir's monochrome cinematography, while terrific, has the unfortunate effect of giving the movie the look and feel of a film noir. This mood is reinforced by the plot, which in fact has no real need of its Algerian War setting; with just a few tweaks to the script and a superficial makeover, *The Unvanquished* could easily play as a thriller free of ties to the OAS (and the war), which may well have yielded better box-office returns. There's one very neat flourish, which occurs late on when the dying Thomas raises his hand as if to move his eyes into the traditional final resting position. In this moment, which was immortalized by British group The Smiths on the sleeve of their 1986 masterpiece *The Queen is Dead*, the film is briefly elevated into something resembling the depiction of existentialist angst it was presumably aiming for all along; Thomas' sense of isolation is so extreme that he feels only he can prevent this final indignity, which of course was one inflicted upon the murdered title character in *Muriel*. Although, on a more pragmatic level, Thomas probably does this to minimize distress for the inhabitants of the house, who include his young daughter.

While the decision to go with the story as it stands undoubtedly hurt the film's chances of success, credit must be given to Delon, that most handsome of blue-eyed matinee idols, for his commitment to a project that dealt with a difficult subject matter, one significantly darker than his core audience would have been used to. With *The Unvanquished*, Delon wasn't afraid to get his hands dirty, and perhaps the boldest aspect of the film, at least in the released version, comes in the form of the female lawyer from mainland France who has come to defend two Algerians the OAS considers to be terrorists. This strongly echoes the real-life situation outlined in *Pour Djamila* (see chapter 3) in which Gisèle Halimi defended Djamila Boupacha, and if we assume that *The Unvanquished*'s Dominique is a proxy for Halimi, then this was a fairly daring move on the part of Delon and his fellow filmmakers. The film also contains a chilling allusion to torture, which occurs when the terrified Dominique lays eyes on the bath in the room where she is to be held captive, only for an OAS member to quickly dispel her fears by demonstrating that the water line isn't connected; this neatly subverts expectations, and in hindsight can be viewed as a clever way in which the filmmakers avoided incurring further censorial wrath. Yet anyone familiar with *Le petit soldat* will instantly understand, and partly feel, the panic experienced by Dominique as the bathtub looms into view.

That Delon's Thomas isn't French also adds an interesting complication, as on more than one occasion he refers to himself as a "foreigner", one who may have joined both the French Foreign Legion and the fanatical OAS yet doesn't seem to identify with France—irrespective of whether Algeria remains French or not. This soldier of (mis)fortune's lack of belief in what the French are doing in Algeria is what leads him to desert in the first place, so he was never going to fare particularly well in a hardcore paramilitary outfit, one which he joins simply because it will earn him enough money to escape Algeria. Thomas' willingness to help the lawyer demonstrates that he values people over political ideals (which aren't even "his"). Alain Delon is good value in his role, as is Massani, the Italian actress who remains best known for her role as the missing Anna in Antonioni's *L'Avventura*, but the film is neither as daring as *Muriel* nor as shocking as *Le petit soldat*, both of which came earlier, and Delon's attempt to depict the Algerian conflict works better as a straightforward thriller than as political commentary.

The OAS was a fairly short-lived operation, yet it left its mark on what was a most turbulent period in French history. It largely achieved this through bringing the war "home" (meaning, to metropolitan France), and the attacks on European soil on the likes of de Gaulle and

Malraux forced a new perspective on French citizens. The Algerian War had hitherto been viewed by those in mainland France as a distant conflict, one which unfolded among palm trees and scorching Saharan heat. All of a sudden, that safe European home felt under threat, as a war which the metropole had previously considered to be alien—although by no means irrelevant—suddenly came crashing into its back yard.

Of course, those who returned to the mainland having served in Algeria would also bring the war home with them, albeit in a more abstract way, and *Muriel*'s Bernard provides a prime example of this. What is arguably the most famous opening line in modern English literature—"The past is a foreign country: they do things differently there"—could easily have been written with Bernard in mind (Hartley, 1953: 9). Bernard contends with his troubled past both *in* and *as* a foreign country, and is quite obviously suffering from some form of Post-traumatic stress disorder (PTSD), many years before the condition was identified. As no-one back in mainland France really wants to hear about the war, this further isolates the disturbed young man, who can think only of his role in Algeria and therefore is unable to relate to the quotidian as discussed by Hélène, Alphonse, et al. In a way it is the OAS that consigns Bernard to his fate, as it is Robert's aggravating presence in Boulogne that eventually drives Bernard to commit (another?) murder, and only by eliminating Robert's map will Bernard finally receive the punishment he so clearly craves for his part in Muriel's death.

For an organization that consisted of so many semi-autonomous cells (including one based in Spain), it seemed most unlikely that the OAS would have been rocked to its core by the taking down of its leader, yet that is exactly what happened. OAS chief Raoul Salan, who incredibly was also France's most decorated soldier on account of his heroics in both world wars, was eventually captured in April 1962 and swiftly put on trial for treason. To the surprise of almost everyone, not least the defendant, Salan narrowly avoided the death penalty and was sentenced to life in prison, although he served just a few years before being pardoned and released in 1968. Salan's conviction spelled the beginning of the end for the organization; a month after the trial, the unlikeliest of scenarios transpired when the OAS signed a ceasefire agreement with the FLN. Although, from an OAS perspective, the war had been lost, a few remained loyal to the cause, and in *Muriel* Robert is an example of one such character who clings to the old dream. With the bulk of its senior members jailed (or sentenced to death by firing squad) in the aftermath of Salan's trial, the OAS limped on for a few years until the 1965 arrest of Gilles Buscia in Marseille effectively snuffed out the organization's nominal existence.

The OAS, whose terror campaign spanned two continents and claimed two thousand lives in the space of one year, may have folded over fifty years ago but, as the ex-members' flowers that appear annually on Raoul Salan's grave prove, the malady lingers on.

Many Unhappy Returns: *Je t'aime, je t'aime* and *Muriel*

Chapter Six

THREE YEARS ELAPSED between *Muriel* and Alain Resnais' next film, and this gap broke the pattern he'd established in releasing a feature every other year. As a follow-up to *Muriel*, *The War Is Over* (*La guerre est finie*, 1966) seemed bound to disappoint, but we should not forget that this film followed not only *Muriel* but also *Hiroshima mon amour* and *Last Year at Marienbad*. Although *Muriel* may not have been as well-received as either of its predecessors, even its biggest critic would concede that it continued the singular path Resnais was forging.

At face value, the black-and-white *The War Is Over* does not demonstrate much progress on the part of its director, appearing as it does to be an exercise in treading water. It's a much more direct film than any of Resnais' previous efforts, which does at least make a change from the complexities of *Hiroshima*, *Marienbad* and *Muriel*, but it nonetheless contains elements, such as a portentous voiceover and one dazzling, rapidly-edited sequence, that mark it out as the work of the same Resnais audiences had become acquainted with over the previous seven years. It also feels quite mainstream, given its straightforward narrative and the casting of Yves Montand as the male lead. While Resnais' prior features were toplined by performers who went on to become household names in France (Emmanuelle Riva, Delphine Seyrig), Montand was an extremely popular leading man when he accepted his part in *The War Is Over*, which meant that this was essentially the first time Resnais had directed an actor who was already an established star at the time of filming. With his appearance opposite Marilyn Monroe in *Let's Make Love* (1960), Montand's celebrity status had extended to Hollywood—although it was not so much the film but rather the stars' rumored off-screen romance that had propelled Montand's face and name into countless newspapers and magazines.

The War Is Over revolves around Montand's Diego Mora, an aging Spanish revolutionary currently living in exile in France. Diego frequently makes risky journeys across the border to his homeland, although his careful use of forged passports keeps him off the authorities' radar. Diego lives with book publisher Marianne, who already has a child from a previous relationship and hopes to start a family with Diego. While returning a passport, Diego discovers that the owner's daughter, Nadine, belongs to a group of young radicals that plans to disrupt the Spanish tourism industry through detonating plastic bombs in Spain; Diego tries to talk them out of this course of action, to no avail. The jaded Diego's dissatisfaction with his own group's work is obvious, and his colleagues feel that he could use some time off. However, they suddenly change their mind and assign him to a job in Barcelona, possibly so they can dispose of an agent they now view as a liability. Diego, who is now known to the police, sets off for Catalonia, and the film ends with Marianne, who has received a tip-off from Nadine, catching a flight to Spain in the hope of intercepting him before he runs into trouble.

Although *The War Is Over* could be described as the first "regular", linear film of Resnais' career, apparently the first draft of the script presented something as complex and fragmented as any of its director's features to that point. The screenplay was by Jorge Semprún, a Spanish author who, like *Muriel* writer Jean Cayrol, was both a French Resistance member and a concentration camp survivor. In a striking parallel with the career of André Malraux—who had also fought in the Resistance—Semprún was later appointed Spain's Minister of Culture, serving for three years in the socialist government that swept away the last remnants of Francoism.

The always-fastidious Resnais reportedly devoted significantly more time to Semprún's script than to those by Duras, Robbe-Grillet and Cayrol for his previous films, and the screenplay was reworked more than once in order to untangle it into a much more direct piece

Jorge Semprún in 2009.

of writing (Monaco, 1979: 96). That Resnais desired a less complicated script signals a deliberate pulling away from the arcane nature of his previous features, and it resulted in an accessible work, one which found a wider audience than any of its predecessors. Semprún, who also served as the film's narrator, received an Oscar nomination for *The War Is Over*, and he would receive the same accolade for his work on Costa-Gavras' landmark feature *Z* (1969), which also starred Yves Montand. It is difficult to work out exactly why Resnais insisted on the streamlining of the screenplay for *The War Is Over*, but perhaps he, much like Montand's Diego in the film, was on the verge of burnout, given that he'd previously directed three hugely demanding, intense films, all of which took an unblinking look at the concept of memory.

Despite its commercial success, *The War Is Over* never quite manages to be a typical genre piece like, say, *The Unvanquished*, but it does play a lot like demystified, diluted Resnais, and as a result feels strangely compromised. After the extremely stylized trio of films that had preceded it, *The War Is Over* both looks and feels a bit *ordinary*, and Resnais' reverse-engineering of Semprún's script resulted in a distinct change of pace for the director.

While *The War Is Over* is certainly one of the least distinctive features in Alain Resnais' early period, it does contain good performances from an interesting array of actors, with Montand's presence augmented by the casting of Canadian Geneviève Bujold and—in a move which reflected the film's status as a Swedish co-production—Ingmar Bergman favorite Ingrid Thulin. *Muriel*'s supporting cast (Martine Vatel, Jean Dasté, Françoise Bertin, Jean-Pierre Kérien) do their best to move things along, and Michel Piccoli is good value in his brief role as a customs officer. With its world of revolutionaries, guerilla warfare, plastic bombs and oppressive regimes, *The War Is Over* has some thematic connections to *Muriel*, and Robert's declaration in the latter that "this is France… the main thing is for every Frenchman to feel alone, frightened… he'll surround himself with barbed wire" appears to elicit a direct response in *The War Is Over*, when Bujold's Nadine declares, "Every man for himself, in his own little corner, is that it? I thought we were more internationalist". Additionally, *Muriel*'s Bernard, for whom the war will *never* be over, would no doubt find something to relate to in Resnais' follow-up to *Muriel*, particularly these sentiments: "You'll spend whole days… trying to rebuild your country in the likeness of your memory".

Study of *The War Is Over*'s script, which is dedicated to Florence Malraux, reveals that the action takes place over three days (plus change) in April 1965, although as in *Muriel* this timeframe is not obvious in the finished film (Semprún, 1966). There is another detail in *The War Is Over* that recalls *Muriel*, which occurs when Diego arrives at an apartment where he expects to find a "Madame Lopez", only to find the female occupant, who identifies herself as "Madame Pluvier", has never heard of the person he's asking for; the bemused inhabitant asks, "Is she a refugee from Algeria? There's a lot of them around here". Given that *The War Is Over* takes place in 1965, could the "refugees" Madame Pluvier speaks of be *Pieds-Noirs* who fled to France from recently-independent Algeria? Curiously, this line isn't present in the published screenplay, so we can therefore assume it to be a late insertion by Resnais (or possibly Semprún) during the film's shoot.

It is difficult to think of a film that seems a less likely candidate for a second instalment than *The War Is Over*, yet both Jorge Semprún and Yves Montand returned for a belated sequel, *Roads to the South* (*Les Routes du sud*, 1978). While Alain Resnais was absent from this endeavor, there was some directorial continuity in the form of Florence Malraux, who joined the production as an AD; the film was directed by Joseph Losey, who had worked with Delphine Seyrig on both *Accident* (1967) and *A Doll's House* (1973).

The War Is Over is certainly not a bad film, but it is far from Alain Resnais' best, and it stands as the weakest of his first four features. However, it is important to have mentioned the film as its place in Resnais' filmography is arguably more important than the movie itself, seeing as it is sandwiched by two oppressively "difficult" films in which the concept of memory is key; we will briefly return to *The War Is Over* once we've considered *Je t'aime, je t'aime* and its relationship with *Muriel*.

Before starting work on *Je t'aime, je t'aime*, Resnais was one of several directors (alongside the likes of Jean-Luc Godard and Agnès Varda) of the portmanteau film *Far from Vietnam* (*Loin du Vietnam*, 1967). Resnais' segment featured a character named Claude Ridder, and Ridder forms a bridge of sorts between Resnais' solo efforts that fall immediately either side of this anthology film; in *Far from Vietnam*, the part of Claude Ridder is performed by *The War Is Over*'s Bernard Fresson (who also appeared in *Hiroshima mon amour*), and Ridder is also the main character in *Je t'aime, je t'aime*, in which he is played by Claude Rich. Like *Muriel*, *Je t'aime, je t'aime* is at its heart an archetypically simple tale, yet it should surprise no-one to learn that Resnais' presentation is anything other than straightforward.

Je t'aime, je t'aime, which translates as *I Love You, I Love You*, begins with failed suicide Claude Ridder being discharged from a Belgian hospital. Upon leaving the building, Ridder is approached by two representatives of a private research facility who offer him the opportunity to partake in an experiment. Ridder, who feels he has little left to lose, agrees. The company has built a time machine, which has been used to send mice back in time, but a human is needed to confirm that the subject did actually visit their past life. Claude is sent back in time—the aim is to place him exactly one year behind the present—and experiences incidents from his past in a jumbled, elliptical and frequently repetitive manner. Among the chaos of the haywire experiment, it is implied that Claude killed Catrine, his terminally ill girlfriend. Ridder does not return to the present promptly, unlike the mice, who have all returned within one minute. The scientists wait for more than an hour, then consider Claude to be lost. The film closes with a shot of a white mouse trapped inside a glass dome.

The immediate fate of *Je t'aime, je t'aime*, which was released in the spring of 1968 to lukewarm box-office returns—it was Resnais' least-attended film to that point—brings us back to Resnais' father-in-law, André Malraux. In February 1968, Malraux's Ministry of Culture had moved to depose Henri Langlois from his post as director of the Cinémathèque Française, and this created much consternation among filmmakers both in France and around the world, with the New Wave directors at the vanguard of the protests. François Truffaut's *Stolen Kisses* (see chapter 4) opens with a shot of the locked gates of the Cinémathèque, and the strength of feeling among Truffaut and his contemporaries saw Langlois reinstated; Malraux, who had instigated Langlois' sacking as a way to exert more control over the Cinémathèque, approved this move but reduced the non-profit institution's funding.

This schism in the French movie industry did not make for an ideal run-in to the 21st Cannes Film Festival, which was due to begin less than a month after the Langlois Affair was resolved, yet by the time the festival opened, France was in the midst of the civil unrest of what is now known as May 68, in which demonstrations, wildcat strikes and riots all contributed to bringing the French economy to a grinding halt. Although Cannes got underway, many of those involved felt that the wider problems in France could not be ignored, and the festival descended into chaos before being curtailed. Truffaut, who had traveled to Cannes in order to discuss the Langlois Affair, was widely viewed as the ringleader of those who had engineered the closure of the event, and his efforts earned him a ban from the festival. *Je t'aime, je t'aime* was supposed to play in competition at Cannes 1968, and although Alain Resnais was actually the one who thought it was best that his film be withdrawn from the festival, the movie was robbed of its ideal launch pad and subsequently slipped between the cracks as France dealt with bigger concerns.

It is hard to argue with film critic Jonathan Rosenbaum, a keen champion of *Je t'aime, je t'aime*, who observed that, upon first viewing, the movie "seems as sharp a decline from *La Guerre est finie*, his previous film, as that one was from *Muriel*" (2020). Yet *seems* is the operative word, as on face value *Je t'aime, je t'aime* appears to be a pale, clumsy imitation of Resnais' greatest triumphs, with its sci-fi leanings—it was written by renowned Belgian fantasy author Jacques Sternberg— seemingly a poor fit for Resnais' well-established preoccupation with memory. That is, until one sees the film again and suddenly realizes that *Je t'aime, je t'aime*'s sci-fi elements dovetail perfectly with its exploration of memory, and time travel allows the film's protagonist— and by extension the viewer—to visit the past, the foreign country that has previously proved so tantalizingly elusive for Resnais' parade of quixotic characters. Resnais may not have been especially interested in science fiction—that *Je t'aime, je t'aime* represented his sole foray into the genre suggests as much—but he did realize that it could be used as a vehicle on which to relay his typical concerns. In *Je t'aime, je t'aime* the time travel concept, which admittedly does prove distracting to an extent, is employed as a framing device, but everything inside that border is instantly recognizable as a continuation of Resnais' previous meditations on the past, which were only interrupted by *The War Is Over*; *Je t'aime, je t'aime* marked the resumption of normal service for Alain Resnais.

The subject matter of *Je t'aime, je t'aime* might make it appear to be a loose-limbed, rather chaotic exercise in raking over the still-smoldering coals of *Hiroshima*, *Marienbad* and *Muriel*, but closer inspection reveals it to be a perfect companion piece to the last of these films. Whether one would *want* to sit through back-to-back screenings of *Muriel* and *Je t'aime, je t'aime* is another matter entirely, given the highly intense nature of both movies and *Je t'aime, je t'aime*'s status as the most downbeat of Resnais' feature films. Hard as it may be to believe, a movie in which white mice are pinged into the past via a time machine really does feel markedly bleaker than a film centering on the torture and murder of a young woman. Although in *Muriel* the past greatly informs the present, there is a clear demarcation between the two times—the characters' abject yearning for the past, among other things, makes this quite clear—whereas *Je t'aime, je t'aime*, in which events from its protagonist's life are frequently embellished and/or conflated, continually wrong-foots the viewer in a way that's as sophisticated as it is unnerving:

> In *Muriel* [...] sequential shifts between past and present serve as a method for addressing a collective sense of shame (the war in Algeria) by acknowledging that the cause of this shame is still present. The memory remains, both in the form of our silence and in the form of tangible suffering, as well as in the form of the moving image. The exploration of memory is more formally complicated in [*Je t'aime, je t'aime*] [...] wherein the recurring presence of the past splinters the present into a cycle of interpretations contingent on a past that no longer has the anchor of subjective certainty. (Vaughan, 2013: 112–113)

Although *Je t'aime, je t'aime*'s brilliance only becomes apparent after several rewatches, most people, quite understandably, will not devote yet more time to a film that has failed to impress them on first viewing, thus partly explaining the film's underwhelming performance at the box office—although the critical reception was generally favorable. Besides being drowned out by the commotion of May 68, *Je t'aime, je t'aime* has an additional problem in that it doesn't *look* quite as appealing as any of Resnais' previous features, all of which had been lensed by virtuoso cinematographer Sacha Vierny, and Jean Boffety's camerawork on *Je t'aime, je t'aime*, while perfectly competent, simply does not carry the same aesthetic appeal; that said, the DVD released by Kino Lorber in 2015 presents a lovely, crisp transfer of a 2K restoration.

Many Unhappy Returns: *Je t'aime, je t'aime* and *Muriel* | 107

The poster for *Je t'aime, je t'aime*'s 2015 home video release.

More than any other film of Resnais', *Je t'aime, je t'aime* is a slow burner, one which eventually clicks into place with the required effort. While the film refuses to give much away on a first—or even second—screening, it does reward repeat viewings, and in this sense it is very different from *Muriel*, which remains largely intransigent no matter how often, or from what angle, you approach it. A first brush with *Je t'aime, je t'aime* can quite easily turn into something of an ordeal, one which the viewer needs to get through before they emerge into something resembling daylight. At times, the film plays like a record that keeps skipping—sometimes back to a moment we've experienced before, occasionally to somewhere altogether new. It's a bit like eavesdropping on someone's REM sleep. If the abstruse *Je t'aime, je t'aime* doesn't yet sound sufficiently confusing, also contemplate that Bernard Fresson—Claude Ridder in *Far from Vietnam*—appears as a character named Bernard, who is a friend of Claude's, who in turn is played by an actor named Claude. There are also cameos from Jorge Semprún and Alain Robbe-Grillet, the respective screenwriters of *The War Is Over* and *Last Year at Marienbad*, alongside *Cahiers du Cinéma* co-founder Jacques Doniol-Valcroze.

To the first-time viewer, the presentation of *Je t'aime, je t'aime* appears elliptical to the point of confrontation, and the maddening, seemingly endless recycling of the same events—most notably Ridder's emergence from a spot of vacation snorkeling—makes the ninety-four minutes feel much, much longer; the lasting irony of the oft-presented snorkeling scene is that Claude will never again come up for air, seeing as he's now endlessly pinballing around time. Ridder moves across the past as if it were a minefield, and the unreliability of memory is highlighted by the presence of the accompanying white mouse, which at one point distracts Claude as it appears in a scenario it couldn't possibly have been part of first time around.

Given the unforgiving, almost hostile nature of *Je t'aime, je t'aime*'s structure, you would almost swear that Resnais is indulging in self-parody, yet the more time you spend with the film, the clearer and more heartbreaking it becomes. James Monaco listed a baker's dozen of points that proved there is a careful pattern to the moments Claude revisits, and the same writer painstakingly produced a timeline for *Je t'aime, je t'aime* from which we can see that the story, in chronological terms, begins on December 7, 1951, and ends on September 3, 1967 (1979: 136–139). The film sees its director's obsession with time and the past enter its terminal stages, and as such *Je t'aime, je t'aime* was more or less Alain Resnais' last word on the subject of the selectivity of memory. The white mice of *Je t'aime, je t'aime* (or their close relations) may have eventually resurfaced in *My American Uncle* (*Mon oncle d'Amérique*, 1980) but, post-1968, Resnais would desist from such taxing forensic examinations of time and memory.

Initial impressions of *Je t'aime, je t'aime* may lead one to conclude that Resnais should perhaps have ceased such investigations with *Muriel*, but closer scrutiny of the former reveals a rigorous, worthy coda to this unique director's exhaustive, expansive study of the individual's relationship with their past. Far from being a grace note, *Je t'aime, je t'aime* is an essential component of Resnais' multi-film study of the past and how we view it; it may immediately appear to be minor Resnais à la *The War Is Over*, but it should not be dismissed by anyone who cares to see where the tracks made by *Muriel*, *Marienbad* and *Hiroshima* ultimately lead. With the endgame that was *Je t'aime, je t'aime*, Alain Resnais' study of memory had reached critical mass, and from then on there would be a noticeable shift in the type of film he would make, and this change of direction will be discussed in chapter 7.

There is no denying that *Je t'aime, je t'aime* is a difficult film to follow, and Resnais' précis of the film ("a man meets a woman— that's all") seems as disingenuous as David Lynch's statement that his own *Inland Empire* (2006) is merely "about a woman in trouble". On reflection, the summaries of these films—both of which might be regarded as highly representative of their directors' respective outputs—are honest, accurate, and about as good as any. It surprises many to learn that *Je t'aime, je t'aime* features around one-third of the number of shots contained in *Muriel* (ibid.: 122). It is even more surprising to discover that the events in *Je t'aime, je t'aime*, although not presented chronologically as in *Muriel*, can be reordered into something resembling a coherent story. It has been suggested that Sternberg wrote the screenplay as a fairly straightforward piece—well, as straightforward as something centering on time travel can be— only for Resnais to drastically rearrange it into the fractured narrative presented in the finished film (Macfarlane, 2014). If we assume this to be the case, then the transition from page to screen provides yet another variation on the methods employed in Resnais' previous two features: *Muriel* saw a complex piece of writing mirrored on the screen, while *The War is Over* had its elaborate screenplay simplified before filming commenced.

If we go with Steve Macfarlane's assumption, *Je t'aime, je t'aime* offered another permutation in that it saw a "straight" piece of writing chopped up and restructured—exactly the sort of process which many incorrectly assumed had been applied to *Muriel*'s screenplay. A different take on the script's genesis has Resnais taking close to a thousand pages of Sternberg's "automatic writing" and distilling them into something roughly a quarter of the size (Rosenbaum, 2018). Whichever version of events you choose to go with, the writing of *Je t'aime, je t'aime* seems as onerous and taxing as anything Resnais had filmed to that point—even though such precise craftsmanship is not immediately obvious.

Unfortunate real-life events frequently prompt us to graft additional meaning onto the films we watch, with two prominent examples being the ways in which the untimely deaths of Brandon Lee and Heath Ledger informed and elevated both *The Crow* (1994) and *The Dark Knight* (2008) respectively. Although no such tragedy haunted *Je t'aime, je t'aime*—an already melancholy work which owes much of its funereal atmosphere to Krzysztof Penderecki's sparse, haunting score—on its initial release, the intervening years have seen the film take on an extra layer of sadness. In *Je t'aime, je t'aime*, Catrine's death prompts her partner to shoot himself, but in reality it was the actress who played Catrine, Olga Georges-Picot, who would take her own life. Three decades on from her starring role in Resnais' film, the stunning Georges-Picot, best known to Anglophone audiences for her post-*Je t'aime, je t'aime* roles in *The Day of the Jackal* (see chapter 5), *The Man Who Haunted Himself* (1970) and Woody Allen's *Love and Death* (1975), leapt to her death from her Paris apartment. Seen through the filter of Olga Georges-Picot's tragic death, *Je t'aime, je t'aime* graduates from extremely moving to almost unbearably sad. Even brief moments of humor can come back to savagely bite us in *Je t'aime, je t'aime*, such as Claude's joke that the scientists should have taught the mice to talk before sending them spinning through time; while this is admittedly quite funny when it occurs in the present, the same quip proves most chilling when it's jarringly replayed, late on the film, as another moment from Claude's past. Resnais' utilization of the same scene to create two contrasting effects is perhaps the best illustration of *Je t'aime, je t'aime*'s brilliance, and the second time the scene occurs proves especially poignant: this is a moment Claude was never meant to relive, but it occurs in his very recent past and therefore puts him agonizingly within touching distance of the present he'll never return to.

Resnais has some gentle fun with the relatively alien Belgian milieu, having Claude teasingly count up as far as the high sixties until the scene cuts abruptly away—therefore stopping just before the number where the French of Belgium and neighboring France bifurcates, in the process denying the viewer the chance to discover if Ridder says seventy in Belgian (*septante*) or Parisian (*soixante-dix*) French. Conversely, Claude visits a doctor who, besides casually mentioning that Ridder did in fact kill Catrine, presents his patient with a bill for *nonante* (ninety)—as opposed to *quatre-vingt-dix*—francs, which clearly identifies the language as Belgian French; of course, the mischievous Resnais could quite easily have chosen a number that is identical in both varieties of the language. *Je t'aime, je t'aime* is crammed full of wordplay, so much so that the English subtitles can't keep up and have to simplify much of it, although an amusing malapropism around stingy/stringy is retained, and the sounds of the Flemish language are briefly used to good effect. There is also a scene in which a character asks Claude, in English, if he speaks English, only for the same character to resurface later on, when he again asks if it is fine to speak in English as he doesn't know French—only this time the man says all of this in French, and continues to converse in the same language. These linguistic games, while diverting, never affect the emotional core of the film.

In the years following *Je t'aime, je t'aime*'s release, Resnais, in an atypically ungracious move, voiced his regret regarding the casting of Georges-Picot, who had beaten a number of other actresses, including Rivette favorite Bulle Ogier, to the role of Catrine (ibid.). It was surprising to learn that Resnais felt Georges-Picot wasn't the best choice for Catrine, as the actress doesn't do much wrong in what is in some ways a more difficult part than Ridder. The troubled, passive Catrine, like Muriel in the film of the same name, is dead before the film begins and therefore exists solely as a ghost, a memory—if she existed at all, seeing as she apparently had no identity papers and most of Claude's friends seem to have been unaware of her. If it wasn't for the time machine, Catrine would be as absent from *Je t'aime, je t'aime* as the title character was from *Muriel*—which is to say, she would be spoken of, but not seen. Claude, who in his past life may not have been as stable as he'd like to think, is as unreliable a narrator as *Muriel*'s Bernard, and it is each of these characters' obsession with a dead woman—be she real or composite—that pushes him into pulling the trigger that will irrevocably change his life. For Claude and Bernard, it is memories that both flay their souls and destroy their common sense. Claude's demise in particular is an especially good fit for what are quite possibly the greatest closing lines in English-language poetry: "This is the way the world ends / Not with a bang but a whimper" (Eliot, 1925: 128).

When Claude goes back in time, he cannot change the past, so he effectively becomes an observer to the story of his romance with Catrine. With this is mind, the Catrine we see is more an avatar than the woman Claude was in love with, and the audience, like Claude, sees Catrine almost as if she's behind glass, and her unhappy life

Olga Georges-Picot (right) in Alain Robbe-Grillet's *Successive Slidings of Pleasure*.

plays out its terrible course. Catrine may be blank, dissociative and rather one-dimensional, but that is hardly Olga Georges-Picot's fault, and the actress' presence becomes more intriguing on subsequent viewings. In many ways Catrine is similar to Delphine Seyrig's A in *Last Year at Marienbad*, as both characters seem to chiefly exist for others—specifically, seemingly unreliable men—to project their own fragile emotions onto. Perhaps Resnais' disappointment lay in the obvious lack of chemistry between the two leads, but the absence of a spark between Claude and Catrine only reinforces the notion that the couple's love, like that of Hélène and Alphonse in *Muriel*, is far more potent as a memory than it was in reality. On the evidence presented in *Je t'aime, je t'aime*, the relationship between Claude and Catrine does not appear to be one worth dying for, and Claude must realize this; the kicker is that he's unable to use this newfound knowledge, as he can't find his way back to the present.

The film's title—which repeats the phrase *je t'aime* presumably so one instance applies to the present, the other to the past—only really makes sense when Claude's present-day *idea* of his love for Catrine is presented. It is this perception that has driven Claude to the point of attempting to eliminate his own map, but his past merely shows us a relationship in which it seems companionship has firmly replaced desire. Given Claude's apparent lack of sincerity, the title could also be read as an allusion to a line in "The Hunting of the Snark"—a poem featured prominently in Jacques Rivette's *Out 1*—in which the Bellman states, "What I tell you three times is true" (Carroll, 1876: 3).

Despite being well over fifty years old, *Je t'aime, je t'aime* neatly avoids looking especially dated, and this is largely due to a key element of its production design: upon hearing the phrase "time machine", most of us will think of a gleaming, metallic, symmetrical contraption adorned with all sorts of wires, levers and buttons, yet *Je t'aime, je t'aime*'s "soft machine" is a large, lumpy, organic-looking mass, one its subject enters before resting on something approximating a beanbag, from where he will be transported to the past. If we consider how the years have not been especially kind to the 1.21 gigawatt-powered DeLorean featured in *Back to the Future* (1985), which at the time was deemed to be cutting edge, then we can see how the carbon-based look of *Je t'aime, je t'aime*'s machine was a wise and prescient choice.

In eschewing a then-modernistic look, Resnais' movie is future-proofed, at least to a degree, and the unsettling design of the machine adds a real edge to the proceedings: is it alive? Sentient? Is Claude, who at one point is shown buried from the neck down in whatever material the contraption consists of, actually absorbed into the machine, thus becoming part of it? A small-scale simulacrum of the device, which features fairly prominently, certainly looks a good deal less organic than the actual machine, and this raises further questions. *Je t'aime, je t'aime*'s longevity is also helped by the film containing no camera effects beyond the jump cuts that occur when Claude and the mouse travel through time, and although the colors in the film possess that hot, vibrant quality that anyone conversant with 1960s cinema will be familiar with, there's little else to date the production beyond the clothes and automobiles on show.

What *Je t'aime, je t'aime* achieves, quite magnificently, is to show the futility that lies in the pursuit of the past, and by extension it retrospectively applies this learning to the characters in *Hiroshima, Marienbad* and, especially, *Muriel*. Although Claude in *Je t'aime, je t'aime* is searching for the past from his position as a man at the end of his rope, it is only his previous, idealized reconstruction of the past that has put him in this situation. Claude, like *Muriel*'s Bernard, certainly has an "obsession with a past that can't come back but won't go away" (Kelley, 2006). The science fiction genre gives Resnais an opportunity to finally send one of his protagonists on the journey so many others have wished for, and the film is as much of an experiment for its director as time travel is for the scientists, even if the two camps have very different aims: Resnais' question concerns whether the past is as perfect as one's memory would have it, while the company simply wants confirmation of its time machine's functionality.

To be reductive for a moment, if *Muriel* is *Last Year at Marienbad* unleashed, then *Je t'aime, je t'aime* is basically *Muriel* with a time machine—only *Je t'aime, je t'aime* provides incontrovertible proof that revisiting the past brings far less happiness than reconstructing it in memory. In doing this, it effectively calls out *Muriel*'s main characters, all of whom look to the past as a sacred space that must be recreated in lieu of it being revisited. There is little doubt that most of *Muriel*'s principal characters (Hélène, Bernard, Alphonse) would eagerly jump into *Je t'aime, je t'aime*'s time machine if given the opportunity, but Claude Ridder is the ultimately unfortunate one who takes the trip, only to find a rather uninspiring love affair, one that has a considerable shortfall to make up if it is to match the one he mourns in the present. *Muriel*'s characters may be living in the past, but *Je t'aime, je t'aime*'s Claude is literally stuck there, and he's very unlikely to recommend the experience; it is a time of return from which there is no return. As Claude repeatedly emerges from an azure ocean, Catrine's oft-replayed question—"was it nice?"—rings especially hollow as *Je t'aime, je t'aime* enters its death spiral. The acedia that facilitated Claude's participation in the experiment has led to a fate much worse than the death he seemingly craved, and we're left with the feel-bad movie of the summer; few films have captured a sense of *Weltschmerz* as intensely as this one.

Considering the many interlocking elements in Alain Resnais' oeuvre, it is only after viewing *Je t'aime, je t'aime* that the place of *The War Is Over* really becomes clear. *Je t'aime, je t'aime* was a project that dated back to 1962, around the time when Resnais was filming *Muriel*, but that it took five years from that point for filming to commence says much about the complexity of *Je t'aime, je t'aime*. Conversely, the relatively simple *The War Is Over*, despite the time and effort devoted to straightening out its screenplay, seemed a fairly direct exercise for Resnais as he limbered up for one last tilt at the memory puzzle. That is not to disparage *The War Is Over*, but it nevertheless feels very much like an "in-between" film, one that doesn't fully stretch the abilities of its maker, who has one eye on something much grander. *The War Is Over* is a much airier, lighter work than any of the films that preceded it, and perhaps Resnais needed to make it in order to decompress and reenergize before undertaking *Je t'aime, je t'aime*, a film that would once again see him plunge headlong into a very intense examination of time and memory. Naturally, *The War Is Over*'s function only became obvious after the release of the haunting, elegiac but chronically undervalued *Je t'aime, je t'aime*, which would be Alain Resnais' last film for six years.

Legacy: *Muriel* and Alain Resnais' Post-1960s Output

Chapter Seven

WE HAVE NOW LOOKED, albeit sometimes very briefly, at each of Alain Resnais' feature films up to and including 1968's *Je t'aime, je t'aime*, and it was after the disappointing reception afforded to that movie that Resnais would take an extended break from filmmaking. When he eventually returned, it was with the Jorge Semprún-penned *Stavisky...* (1974), a film that marked a departure from the director's established working practices, given that it appeared following a break that was three times as long as was typical for Alain Resnais, and it was the first feature film of his to see a returning screenwriter—although *Muriel*'s Jean Cayrol had previously worked with Resnais on the short-form documentary *Night and Fog*. Resnais' first five feature films all had different writers, but this tradition ended when Semprún, the Oscar-nominated screenwriter of *The War Is Over*, was tasked with tackling the strange story of naturalized French embezzler Alexandre Stavisky, whose crooked dealings had brought the French government to its knees. A big question mark remains over Stavisky's suicide by gunshot, given the estimated distance the fatal bullet traveled (around 10 feet), which prompted irreverent satirical newspaper *Le Canard enchaîné* to quip that the act must have been performed by a man with "a very long arm" (Legrand, 2014).

As with the earlier film Semprún had written for Resnais, *Stavisky...* (the ellipsis in the title implies there's more to the affair, which there almost certainly is) starred a household name, and the presence of Jean-Paul Belmondo, along with Stephen Sondheim's jaunty score, contributed to the film's commercial success; in France—where box office is measured in terms of tickets sold as opposed to a financial total—the film racked up over one million entries, making it Resnais' biggest hit to that point. The advertising posters for *Stavisky...*, in which the image of Belmondo—who had commissioned Semprún's script—unsurprisingly figures prominently, give the impression of a straightforward crime drama, but it seems that Resnais was incapable of making a *completely* mainstream film, and anyone familiar with the director's work wouldn't have been too surprised by his non-linear presentation of the Stavisky Affair, a political scandal so great it eventually toppled a government. For apparently no good reason other than to possibly pre-empt Stavisky's demise, there is a lingering shot of a dead mouse lying on the ground, which although unlikely to be one from *Je t'aime, je t'aime*—it's the wrong color, for one thing—seems a strange detail to include; however, there is a definite sighting of one of *Je t'aime, je t'aime*'s time travelers in the form of Claude Rich, who turns up as an inspector on Stavisky's tail.

As with *The Unvanquished*, the presence of an A-list star does not obfuscate the *slightly* off-center nature of *Stavisky...* but, in contrast to Alain Delon's poorly-received venture, the paying public seemingly had no major objections to Resnais' flourishes. The overall impression one takes away from *Stavisky...* is that Jorge Semprún, although a great writer, wasn't an ideal fit for Alain Resnais, as their two collaborations stand as the most unremarkable films in their director's résumé. The film is notable as the first of several Resnais films to feature Gérard Depardieu, who briefly appears as an inventor who claims to have created the Matriscope—a device that can determine the sex of a baby in the womb. *Stavisky...* also marked the only time Resnais worked with the late Michael Lonsdale, who isn't given much to do as Stavisky's trusted physician; in the same year, Lonsdale would reunite with his *The Day of the Jackal* co-star Olga Georges-Picot in *Marienbad* writer Alain Robbe-Grillet's haptic, experimental art film *Successive Slidings of Pleasure* (*Glissements progressifs du Plaisir*, 1974), a far cry from the fairly orthodox period piece that was *Stavisky....* Four years before his death, the intensely private Lonsdale—who frequently dropped the "a" from his first name when billed in French productions—published his memoirs, in which he revealed that he had fallen in love with Delphine

Sandrine Kiberlain and André Dussollier in *Life of Riley*.

Seyrig: "It was her or nothing, and that's why at 85 I'm still unmarried" (2016, as cited in Bergan, 2020).

Resnais made just one other film in the 1970s—the English-language *Providence* (1977), which may have *looked* like a dusty old chamber piece yet proved to be anything but; while it wasn't quite as popular as *Stavisky...*, it still sold more tickets than both *Je t'aime, je t'aime* and *Muriel*. Scripted by English playwright David Mercer, hitherto best known for *Morgan—A Suitable Case for Treatment* (1966), *Providence*—which won seven Césars (the French equivalent of the Academy Award), including best film and best director—was another movie in which the lead character looked back on their life, but it wasn't nearly as elusive as Resnais' earlier musings on memory. Still, there's much to enjoy, as John Gielgud's embittered, ailing writer spends a dark night of the soul constructing scenes in his head, all of which center on his nearest and not so dearest, who include Dirk Bogarde as yet another Claude.

There are slight echoes of *Je t'aime, je t'aime* in *Providence*, especially in the moments when characters wander into scenes they're obviously not supposed to be in, and the shot of a town being demolished explicitly recalls the Boulogne of *Muriel*. The blurring of the lines between reality and fantasy is a key theme here, as "real" people mingle with imaginary beings in setups which explicitly call out the unreliability of memory. *Morgan* star David Warner (dubbed by Gérard Depardieu in the French version of *Providence*) was among the highly distinguished cast but, more than any of Resnais' other post-*Muriel* films, *Providence* was crying out for the presence of Delphine Seyrig—then again, what wasn't? Seyrig would have been a perfect fit for the role played by Elaine Stritch, who doesn't appear quite tuned in to the game Mercer and Resnais are playing, thus leaving a glaring Seyrig-shaped hole in the film; Ellen Burstyn, in the other major female role, fares much better.

Some of *Providences*'s many fantasy scenes feature an unusual design element in the form of painted backdrops, a technique Resnais would later return to when he was fully focused on legitimate theater. In *Providence*, Resnais may well be answering his critics via Gielgud's Clive Langham, who seethes, "It's been said about my work that the search for style has often resulted in a want of feeling"; Resnais' reputation as an aloof, somewhat cold filmmaker was one unfairly applied, as few if any of his films, *Providence* included, could be said to lack an emotional core. That said, there is an atypically mean-spirited element to *Providence*, although such misanthropic leanings could be more a product of Mercer than Resnais. At times, the writing recalls that of Harold Pinter, and this feeling is underlined by the presence of Bogarde, an actor who starred in two of the three films Pinter wrote for *Roads to the South*'s Joseph Losey (a fourth collaboration between playwright and director—an adaptation of Marcel Proust's *Remembrance of Things Past*—never made it to the screen).

Yet *Providence*'s invariably unlikeable characters do not impede one's enjoyment of what is an immaculate, hugely satisfying piece of work. One thing that stands out—or rather doesn't—in *Providence* is that it at no point feels like a director working in another language; it's by no means uncommon for a filmmaker to misfire when they move outside of their first language, but *Providence*, which may actually go down as Resnais' outright funniest work, signaled a director who was savvy to such pitfalls. In his autobiography, which was published just a couple of years after *Providence*'s release, John Gielgud credits

AD Florence Malraux, who was perfectly fluent in English, for her significant contribution to what the revered stage actor referred to as "the most exciting film I have ever made" (1979: 195–198).

As the 1980s dawned, Resnais directed what can be considered to be his last truly "difficult" film in *My American Uncle*, which stands as something of an anomaly in his post-1968 output. The film is underpinned by the philosophies of neurobiologist Henri Laborit, an eminent doctor known for his key role in the development of the antipsychotic drug chlorpromazine. Laborit appears as himself and presents what can be described as a lecture on the physiology of the human brain and the different types of animal behavior: inhibition, consumption, escape, and struggle. Laborit's presentation is punctuated by scenarios in which several characters, including Gérard Depardieu's René and Nicole Garcia's Janine, play out situations which help illustrate the points being made. Partly filmed in Alain Resnais' home department of Morbihan, *My American Uncle* was a surprise hit, with ticket sales in France exceeding those for *Stavisky...* and indeed anything else Resnais had made to that point, and its unlikely record would stand for many years. The movie also enjoyed a long run in American cinemas, although it would prove to be the last film of Resnais' to receive US-wide distribution. There appears to be a certain arbitrariness to the film's great success—in many ways it isn't any more accessible than *Muriel*, *Je t'aime, je t'aime* or *Last Year at Marienbad*, and it is certainly a good deal less mainstream than either *Stavisky...* or *The War Is Over*, yet *My American Uncle* outgrossed every one of these films.

While *My American Uncle* is a slightly tricky film to navigate, it is in no meaningful way concerned with memory, although it is infused with a melancholy that makes it feel like a relative of *Je t'aime, je t'aime* and, by extension, *Muriel*; its relationship to the former is quite explicit in the form of René's attempted suicide, while the latter is recalled via Janine's unhappy love affairs. Another link to *Je t'aime, je t'aime* comes in the form of the white rodents that are used to elucidate Henri Laborit's points; at one stage, a humanoid mouse appears, to quite comic effect, although such a sight presents us with the slight possibility that this could be a chimera of *Je t'aime, je t'aime*'s Claude Ridder and the mouse who accompanied him on that film's ill-fated journey through time.

In *My American Uncle* (the title alludes to a mythical character who can solve all of one's problems), the presence of the humanoid mouse may help to illuminate what was previously an inexplicable image in *Je t'aime, je t'aime*, in which a figure in a business suit and some sort of lizard mask appears near Ridder. While this moment can be readily attributed to dream logic, one of the theories Laborit expounds in *My American Uncle* implies that *Je t'aime, je t'aime*'s mysterious masked figure might have some connection to the reptilian brain. Although it can take a little while to tune in to *My American Uncle*'s modus operandi, the vignettes enacted by Depardieu, Garcia et al. are very effective in illustrating some of Laborit's key ideas:

> A major role of the brain is to organize behaviors, i.e., action. There is inhibition of action when behaviors become impossible, and this is deleterious to health. This happens when an instinctive behavior (such as fight or flight) is impossible, when acting is useless, when a danger cannot be predicted, or when no previous response pattern exists to direct action. In these situations, a brain system, the *système inhibiteur de l'action*, or behavioral inhibition system (BIS), is activated and stimulates the neuroendocrine responses that were described by Walter Cannon in the 1920s and Hans Selye in the 1930s and 1940s. [...] Responses to one's environment, when dysfunctional, become toxic, as Laborit studied in the 1950s in the field of anesthesia. He later studied the behavior of rats and concluded that inhibition of action induced pathogenic mechanisms. He observed that humans have ancestral instinctive behavioral responses that are not adapted to the modern societal milieu. His aim was to explain biology and behavior at each of the different levels of functioning, from cell to society. (Kunz, 2014)

We can think of Alain Resnais' work in feature films as being divided into three distinct phases: up to and including *Je t'aime, je t'aime*; from *Stavisky...* through *Love Unto Death* (*L'Amour à mort*, 1984); and from *Mélo* on. There's a quite uneven split evident in this divvying up of the score of films, which works out as 5–5–10, forming a Fibonacci sequence (of sorts) that I'm sure must represent a deliberate pattern as much as that found in James Monaco's tally of the repeated scenes in *Je t'aime, je t'aime*. That said, separating Resnais' films at exactly the halfway point also works, seeing as those from film number eleven (*Mélo*) on all fit quite comfortably into the one camp. While we have not yet looked at all of the films in Resnais' "middle" period, let alone those in his third phase, it is fair to say that the second tranche of films in his career is the only one in which no particular theme emerged.

Yet it is in this stretch of films that *My American Uncle* appeared, and it stands as what is almost certainly Resnais' strongest post-*Je t'aime, je t'aime* movie (although *Providence* is also a contender for that title). It is tempting to attach such a label to *My American Uncle* merely on the grounds of its reasonably challenging nature, but none of Resnais' films could be said to lack ambition; he never made an uninteresting film in his career, and even Alain Resnais on an off day is preferable

The poster for the 2018 re-release of *My American Uncle*.

to most other filmmakers on top form. What marks out *My American Uncle* is that it feels more driven, focused and rigorous than many of the other films in Alain Resnais' post-1968 work; you can't help but think that the presence of a brilliant mind like Henri Laborit forced Resnais to up his game, so much so that he was pushed to creative heights he hadn't experienced since around the time Cannes was shut down in the late 60s.

My American Uncle was written by Jean Gruault, who had scripted five of François Truffaut's movies and would go on to write Resnais' next two films, *Life is a Bed of Roses* (*La vie est un roman*, 1983) and *Love Unto Death*. The last of Gruault's collaborations with Truffaut, *The Green Room* (*La Chambre verte*, 1978), has a strong thematic connection with Resnais' memory films—particularly *Muriel*, a movie Truffaut was initially quite ambivalent about. *The Green Room*, which is frequently dismissed as one of its esteemed director's lesser films, is based on three of Henry James' stories, with *The Altar of the Dead* forming the main basis of Gruault's adaptation. In a move which highlights the personal nature of the project, Truffaut himself stars as Julien, an obituary writer and widower who turns an abandoned chapel into a monument to the dead. Julien has reached that point where life is one big funeral, and he now knows more people in the ground than on the surface; in line with this trend, his eerie, elaborate tribute space, which is full of photographs and candles, starts to take up more and more of his time. In a memorable scene, Julien castigates a priest for serving up empty platitudes to mourners; what they really need, argues Julien, is for their loved ones to return. A few words for the dead won't really cut it.

Julien has no access to the time machine of *Je t'aime, je t'aime*, but there is no doubt that he, like *Muriel*'s main characters, would take a trip in it given half a chance. In the absence of such technology, all Julien can do is worship the dead, and he elevates them to a status that no living person—not even Nathalie Baye's comely Cécilia—could ever hope to match. In essence, Julien has created a private religion, one that has the veneration of the dead as its central commandment. Eventually, Julien reaches the terminus of his death trip, collapsing under the strain of it all and duly joining those he's devoted so much time to.

Although *The Green Room* is ultimately rather predictable, it contains a depiction of one man's obsession with the dead to rival the one seen in *Muriel*. Julien could quite easily be an older version of Bernard, and both characters view the living as vastly inferior to those who have been immortalized through death; both Julien's wife and Muriel are suspended in a world without end, and the living versions of both women could almost certainly never measure up to their idealized counterparts. *The Green Room* plays like the tail end of something Resnais began with *Muriel*, and it holds a curious place in Jean Gruault's career, marking his final collaboration with Truffaut but antedating his work with Resnais, yet it owes a debt to a type of film Alain Resnais had long since abandoned. Both Truffaut and Gruault seemed to cast their eyes toward *Muriel* while working on *The Green Room*, and the prominent casting of *Muriel*'s Jean Dasté, as Julien's editor, only reinforces such a link.

The elegiac *The Green Room* is arguably the most underappreciated and least-seen of Truffaut's films, and it reminds us of how adept he was in front of the camera; he had given a similarly engaging lead performance in the Gruault-penned *The Wild Child* (*L'enfant sauvage*, 1970), another of Truffaut's less-lauded films. His ability as an actor went largely unrecognized—or perhaps it was simply eclipsed by his talent as a director—but he was good value in all of the films he performed in, including his Oscar-winning *Day for Night* (*La nuit americaine*, 1973) and Steven Spielberg's *Close Encounters of the Third Kind* (1977). *The Green Room* makes for especially sad viewing given that Truffaut would die just six years later, although he still had time to squeeze in four more films between its release and his premature death at the age of fifty-two. Mathieu Amalric, who starred in two of Alain Resnais' last three films, cited *Je t'aime, je t'aime* as a direct influence on *The Blue Room* (*La Chambre bleue*, 2014), a movie that resembled *The Green Room* in both its title and the fact that its director was also its star ("Mathieu Amalric", 1:25–1:35). Amalric is one of just two actors to hold the dual status of Resnais star and James Bond villain, the other being Michael Lonsdale.

Jean Gruault's second film with Alain Resnais, *Life is a Bed of Roses*, presents three interconnected stories across as many eras, with a castle in the Ardennes Forest serving as the shared setting. It is quite possibly the most confounding of Resnais' features, and its presentation of the ancient and the modern sees it play like a mash-up of the work of Resnais contemporary Éric Rohmer (who, like Resnais, was another "late starter" in feature films), a feeling emphasized by the presence of Rohmer favorite Marie Rivière (there's also a splash of Jacques Demy's *Once Upon a Time* thrown in). The film has some interesting moments, but no perceptible point—although further scrutiny may well yield a better understanding. One strange twist, at least for Anglophone audiences, occurs in the film's title being translated more literally ("life is a fairytale") when it is said toward the end of the film, thus robbing a subtitle-dependent audience of the moment when the title is mentioned in the dialogue. In what could be construed as a nod to the Boulogne of *Muriel*, one of *Life is a Bed of Roses*' characters glibly mentions that "only happy people can build a harmonious city".

The third and final collaboration between Gruault and Resnais, *Love Unto Death*, touched on themes familiar to both writer and director in its exploration of the two keywords in the title: a couple's incipient relationship is suddenly halted when the man, played by Pierre Arditi, suddenly dies, although he soon comes back to life. Not for the first time, Resnais dealt with a time of return that would lead to unexpectedly complicated consequences, and the film's basic concept, a riff on W. W. Jacobs' short story *The Monkey's Paw*, provided a framework which would allow both director and screenwriter to examine yet another possibility: that of the revenant.

If the time machine of *Je t'aime, je t'aime* is a response to the call of *Muriel*, the resurrection in *Love Unto Death* similarly answers Gruault's *The Green Room*, as it seems to provide the ideal solution to Julien's problem. Although what would he really think if the dead did return? How could he then continue to worship them? Julien, and *Muriel*'s Bernard for that matter, belong to the group Lewis Hyde referred to as "the trapped who have come to enjoy their cage" (1986: 16). With its metaphysical musings, in which unlikely clergywoman Fanny Ardant (in the second of three consecutive roles for Resnais) plays a key part, *Love Unto Death* again feels a lot like Resnais doing Rohmer, although *Muriel*'s ghosts are also present in the form of composer Hans Werner Henze and actor Jean Dasté, who plays the doctor who diagnoses the death. *Love Unto Death* was released just a matter of weeks before the death of François Truffaut and in the same month that Ardant and Truffaut's daughter Josephine would turn one year old. Not for the first or last time, external circumstances would imbue a Resnais film with an unwanted tinge of sadness.

The films from *Stavisky...* through *Love Unto Death* had certainly seen Alain Resnais change things up, but it was his first film following the latter that set him on the path he would stick to, fairly closely, for the rest of his career. *Mélo* was Resnais' first adaptation of a play (it's based on a 1929 work by Henri Bernstein), and it saw the director again work with the core group of actors from *Life is a Bed of Roses* and *Love Unto Death*. Like its predecessor, *Mélo* is a downbeat work, one which recalls *Muriel* in both its theme of lost love and the supposition of what might have happened had a certain letter not been received (which neatly inverts the situation at the end of *Muriel*); Resnais' old, familiar concerns surface explicitly when André Dussollier's Marcel is heard to lament how he's haunted by the past. In what may be a nod to *Love Unto Death*, Pierre Arditi's character suddenly collapses with a terrible head pain, except this time he makes a prompt and full recovery. In continuing to use the same actors for multiple, consecutive films, the director clearly broke from the pattern he'd established in the 1960s and 70s:

> Resnais dramatically reversed his practice regarding actors in the mid-1980s. Until then his accepted rule had been to avoid repeating the same headliners multiple times. Only Delphine Seyrig had been the star of two consecutive films, *Last Year at Marienbad* and *Muriel*, while others had to be satisfied with a unique collaboration, such as Emmanuelle Riva in *Hiroshima mon amour*, Yves Montand in *The War Is Over* or Nicole Garcia in *My American Uncle*. With its lead roles offered to Laura Benson and Adolph Green, *I Want to Go Home* was the last film to meet this model. The quartet formed by Sabine Azéma, Fanny Ardant, Pierre Arditi and André Dussollier, inducted with *Life is a Bed of Roses*, *Love Unto Death* and *Mélo*, then tightened up to the duo Azéma–Arditi for *Smoking* [1993] and *No Smoking* [1993], gave way in *Same Old Song* [1997] to a new quartet

> where Azéma, Arditi and Dussollier were joined by Lambert Wilson. In many cases, it was understood from the outset, before the writing of the original screenplay or the selection of the work to be adapted, that the film should include roles for the members of this quartet. [...] This choice of quartet and a handful of other performers invited two or three times in a row, such as Anne Consigny, Mathieu Amalric or Michel Vuillermoz, emerges all the more in the theatrical adaptations [...] *Private Fears in Public Places* [2006] and [...] *Life of Riley* [2014]. (Thomas, 2016)

From *Mélo* on, Alain Resnais would display a predilection for theatrical pieces—seven of his last ten films were based on works that had originally been presented on the stage—and, as the above quote points out, Resnais would continue to use the same nucleus of actors (for more detail on Resnais' casting habits, please see Appendix B). This is much in line with the concept of the theatrical troupe, and such practice aligns with Resnais' later preference for theater. To briefly consider the minority of post-*Mélo* films that weren't based on stage works: *I Want to Go Home* (surprisingly, its original title) was a culture-clash comedy centering on an American cartoonist's trip to France; *Wild Grass* (*Les herbes folles*, 2009) adapted Christian Gailly's 1996 book *L'incident* into a ridiculously fun shaggy dog story, and also marked the first time that Resnais, who'd frequently used novelists as screenwriters, had actually based a film on a novel; and *Same Old Song* (*On connaît la chanson*) used a variety of popular songs to convey the generally hidden emotions of its characters.

I Want to Go Home, which cast Broadway lyricist Adolph Green as the cantankerous visitor abroad, was a resounding failure at the box office, and its poor sales made it Resnais' least commercially successful film. To put this in context, *I Want to Go Home*'s ticket sales for the whole of France totaled less than 40% of *Mélo*'s (middling) Paris admissions. *I Want to Go Home*'s poor reception may have had something to do with its title, as it's not the easiest one for monoglot French speakers to ask for at the ticket booth. It didn't help that the majority of this fish-out-of-water tale's dialogue was in English, although, as is usual

Sandrine Kiberlain in *Life of Riley*.

in France for films that aren't in French to begin with, a dub was created for the Gallic market. However, this version defeated much of the film's main point, which was that the principal character couldn't speak French; for once, we had a Resnais character who quite literally couldn't express himself, which at least gave him a proper excuse from opening up emotionally.

With much of the comedy derived from this language barrier scenario, the French dub presents us with the nonsensical spectacle of a late scene in which the main character is desperately pleading for someone, anyone, to speak English—confusingly, the soundtrack has reverted to its original audio at this point—yet the same character has been speaking fluent French in many of the scenes prior to this point. Such a scenario may have made—ahem—sense within the logic of *Je t'aime, je t'aime*, but *I Want to Go Home*'s dubbing could easily be used as exhibit A by those fiercely opposed to the process. Most directors, at least those of what is widely considered to be arthouse fare, wish for their films to be viewed solely in their original-language versions (with the addition of subtitles where necessary), and France is a country where the director, reassuringly, always has final cut, so it is possible that Resnais had not properly anticipated the distortion of his vision via some very awkward dubbing, which ironically was created for the domestic market. For all that, it is doubtful if *Providence* would have achieved its considerable success without its French dub track, which was assembled with great care.

It is easy to see why *I Want to Go Home* flopped in its native country, but the original-language version is a strong and very funny work which marked Resnais' best film since *My American Uncle*, which meant that he'd bookended the 1980s with two films which saw him on sparkling form. There was a sense that the three movies prior to *I Want to Go Home* saw Resnais performing within himself, and in the context of his entire filmography these works look a lot like dry runs for his later theatrical adaptations; compared to the likes of *Muriel*, *Providence*, *Last Year at Marienbad* and *Je t'aime, je t'aime*, they certainly should be viewed as pale, relatively minor Resnais. Among the frivolity of *I Want to Go Home*—an early marker of Resnais' fondness for farce and its highly contrived nature—there's a moment in which the frustrated protagonist, finding himself in a bedroom with two women (naturally), finally blows a fuse and yells, "What's wrong with you people? Can't you keep your problems to yourselves?" While this happens during a comical scene, many of Resnais' previous leading characters—most pertinently those in *Muriel*—might feel that this stinging rebuke is aimed at them. *I Want to Go Home*, whose witty screenplay was written by American cartoonist Jules Feiffer, most certainly did not deserve its box office fate.

At the other end of the commercial spectrum was *Same Old Song* (ironically, it was anything but), a film which owed much to its dedicatee, the English dramatist Dennis Potter. Although it wasn't based on an existing text, this UK co-production was clearly the work of someone very much in love with the theater. A film crammed with hit songs, which the characters spontaneously, briefly lip-synced to à la Potter in order to express otherwise-unsaid feelings, *Same Old Song* tore up the domestic box office to the tune of over 2.5 million admissions, easily becoming Resnais' biggest hit as it made roughly twice the ticket sales of *My American Uncle*. The film's huge success can be attributed to several factors: its catchy soundtrack of popular

French tunes; the impressive ensemble cast, which included the likes of Jane Birkin, Jean-Pierre Darroussin, André Dussollier, and *Muriel*'s Françoise Bertin; and, perhaps most significantly of all, its highly accessible nature. It's a hugely enjoyable film, although it isn't among Alain Resnais' *very* best; furthermore, the gap in quality between *Same Old Song* and *I Want to Go Home* is by no means as great as the wildly contrasting box-office figures might suggest. *Same Old Song* stands as the plainest depiction of the alexithymia that has blighted many of its director's characters, and as such it is an unusually direct film for Resnais—well, as direct as a film concerning people skirting around their feelings can be; later, *Private Fears in Public Places* (*Cœurs*) would cover similar ground. The chasm between what we think and what we say had been a preoccupation of Resnais' that dated all the way back to the time of *Muriel*:

> You can describe anxiety from the outside. But there is mental life. I really liked Hitchcock's *Vertigo* [1958]. Filming what's going on in your head is not subjectivism, it is another realism. You are here, drinking your tea. But at the same time different things are going on in your head. Everyone lives in their fantasies. This is what makes communication between beings so difficult. (Bounoure, 1962)

Almost thirty-five years before *Same Old Song*, Alain Resnais presented a radical, egalitarian take on the importance of *Muriel*'s entire cast of characters, proposing that "ideally they would all appear to be equally interesting. Even a figure seen in the street, one must be able to think that [...] it was his story that would have been the most interesting" (ibid.). However, it wasn't until *Same Old Song* that we saw Resnais put this theory into practice; in what is perhaps the film's most interesting and least orthodox scene, the camera eavesdrops on two female friends having a heart-to-heart in a restaurant, before it moves on to the table of two of the film's firmly established characters. We never see these two women outside of this restaurant scene, and it proves Resnais' assertion that anyone else on the margins (or even outside) of the frame—such as *Muriel*'s title character—could be just as interesting as a film's main personas. With this scene in *Same Old Song*, Resnais walked the walk in what can be viewed as a counter to the typical placing of peripheral characters in cinema and television. In David Foster Wallace's byzantine novel *Infinite Jest*, one of its hundreds of characters analyzes this concept in relation to the sitcom *Cheers* (1982–1993), considering:

> the myriad thespian extras [...], not the center-stage Sam and Carla [...], but the nameless patrons always at tables, filling out the bar's crowd, concessions to realism, always relegated to back and foreground; and always having utterly silent conversations: their faces would animate and mouths move realistically, but without sound; only the name-stars at the bar itself could audibilize. [...] [T]hese fractional actors, human scenery, could be seen (but not heard) in most pieces of filmed entertainment. [...] [W]hat a miserable fucking bottom-rung job that must be for an actor, to be sort of human furniture, figurants [...] they're called, these surreally mute background presences whose presence really revealed that the camera, like any eye, has a perceptual corner, a triage of who's important enough to be seen and heard v. just seen. (1996: 834–835)

In its original context, this passage represents *Infinite Jest* at its most meta, given that Wallace's novel gives numerous figurants their chance to shine. The year after *Infinite Jest*'s first publication, Resnais' attempt in *Same Old Song* to rescue the figurant from their silent obscurity is a rather bold move in what is otherwise a very straightforward film, and in a way it echoes the few off-kilter moments that were sprinkled throughout the largely mainstream *Stavisky....* While this moment doesn't prove especially distracting, it nevertheless hints at the tantalizing possibility of a highly experimental version of *Same Old Song*, one in which there are *no* central characters, lurking beneath the slick surface of Alain Resnais' most popular—and most populist—movie.

Sandwiched between Resnais' least and most successful films was his adaptation of English playwright Alan Ayckbourn's *Intimate Exchanges*, an unusual stage work in that it has sixteen possible endings

Legacy: *Muriel* and Alain Resnais' Post-1960s Output | 133

Alain Resnais (far right) on set with the cast of *You Ain't Seen Nothin' Yet*.

depending on the various choices its characters make, such as whether to smoke a cigarette. Resnais distilled the action down to five hours that were then spread across two films, *Smoking* and *No Smoking*, which were intended to be consumed back to back, much like both volumes of Lars von Trier's *Nymphomaniac* (2013). Ayckbourn's play is set in his native England, and Resnais decided to keep the setting but had all of the dialogue rewritten in French, and the whole thing was filmed on a Paris soundstage that quite deliberately makes no pretense at looking or sounding like the real locations, making the whole endeavor look quite literally like a filmed play; that there are no exterior settings in the script heightens the sense that naturalism is being completely rejected. Moreover, all of the parts are played by just two performers, Pierre Arditi and Resnais' second wife Sabine Azéma.

If anyone lacks the level of suspension of belief required for this setup, it's not too different from the one featured in *The Day of the Jackal*, which would have us believe that French government ministers only speak in cut-glass-accented English. Although loosely marketed as a comedy, *Smoking/No Smoking* contains moments of real pathos, especially in its latter stages, and it stands as Resnais' starkest illustration of the overall importance of seemingly trivial choices. The movie was successful, netting best film, best actor and Resnais' second best director award at the Césars, and it would not be the last time Resnais would turn to the work of Ayckbourn. The writers of the film, (then) real-life couple Agnès Jaoui and Jean-Pierre Bacri, were also winners at the Césars for their work on *Smoking/No Smoking*; Jaoui and Bacri also penned *Same Old Song*, which likewise won best film and best screenplay among the seven Césars it swept up at the 1998 ceremony.

Following *Same Old Song*, Resnais appeared to attempt a similar trick with *Not on the Lips* (*Pas sur la bouche*, 2003), a faithful adaptation of André Barde and Maurice Yvain's 1925 operetta. Resnais retained the original libretto and added *Amélie* (*Le fabuleux destin d'Amélie Poulain*, 2001) stars Isabelle Nanty and Audrey Tautou to its cast of otherwise usual suspects, and the film met with fair commercial success. Its overt theatricality, Jazz Age setting and frequent bursts of sung dialogue place it somewhere between *Mélo* and *Same Old Song*, but by the end *Not on the Lips* descends into a proto-Ayckbournian farce, one in which, unusually for Resnais, the times when the action takes place are clearly signaled onscreen.

An adaptation of Ayckbourn's *Private Fears in Public Places*—another work centering on the unsaid—followed, to similar box-office numbers as *Not on the Lips*, before Resnais briefly broke off from adaptations of stage work to film *Wild Grass*. Resnais turned his attention back to theater with his penultimate film, *You Ain't Seen Nothin' Yet*, a meta-adaptation of two plays by noted French playwright Jean Anouilh; it was Anouilh who had dramatized *Madame de…*, the best-known novel by Louise de Vilmorin, a writer who, in the last years of her life, became André Malraux's companion. Alain Resnais was ninety years old when *You Ain't Seen Nothin' Yet* hit cinemas, and although the film did not perform well commercially—only *I Want to Go Home* ranks lower in terms of the box-office takings of Resnais' films—its director showed no signs of slowing down.

You Ain't Seen Nothin' Yet was a film I was greatly looking forward to, but when I finally caught up with the film—annoyingly, I'd missed its initial theatrical run and had to settle for watching it on Blu-ray—I considered it to be something of a disappointment, one which resoundingly failed to deliver on the fun promised by both its cast and premise. *You Ain't Seen Nothin' Yet* arrived on the back of the terrific *Wild Grass* and featured many of the same performers, which no doubt led to high expectations for Resnais' Anouilh adaptation(s). As has already been discussed, Alain Resnais' films often refuse to give much away on a first viewing, so it may well be that the case with *You Ain't Seen Nothin' Yet* is, well, you ain't seen nothin' yet—unless you're willing to go a few more rounds with it. Given Resnais' track record, something tells me it may well be a film worth persevering with.

For what would turn out to be his last film, Resnais once again looked across the English Channel to Alan Ayckbourn, whose *Life of Riley* would become the third of the British dramatist's works to be adapted by Resnais. As with the film of *Private Fears in Public Places*, which carried the original title *Cœurs* ("Hearts"), Resnais' *Life of Riley* (*Aimer, boire et chanter*), whose French title translates as "Love, Drink and Sing", reverted back to the title of Ayckbourn's play for its release in English-speaking territories. At the time of Alain Resnais' death in 2014 at the age of ninety-one, he was working on filming a fourth Ayckbourn play, *Arrivals and Departures*, and a first draft of the screenplay had been completed.

Resnais would not live to witness *Life of Riley*'s general release in cinemas, which occurred just a few weeks after his death, although he did see the film win a Silver Bear at the 2014 Berlin Film Festival; the particular accolade awarded to *Life of Riley* was the Alfred Bauer Prize, which was rebranded in 2020 following allegations of Nazi collaboration made against the man who lent his name to the award. Being a Resnais adaptation of an Ayckbourn play, *Life of Riley* unsurprisingly recalls both *Smoking/No Smoking* and *Private Fears in Public Places*, but it also harks back to the distant past and *Muriel* via one particular detail: the title character is never seen, yet remains at the center of the film. One way in which *Life of Riley* most definitely *didn't* recall *Muriel* was in its number of edits, as it consisted of just:

> one hundred and thirty-eight shots excluding credits, that is to say a style based on unusually long shots (half of the dialogue scenes are even planned as a sequence

shot). Only the main camera movements are noted, but it is understood from the outset that the camera, which is as light as possible, will hardly move except according to the movements of the actors. Resnais and [screenwriter Laurent] Herbiet add stage directions [...] [and] go all out, notably with [...] the whole range of optical transitions (iris openings and closures, fades to black, crossfades, etc.). Unlike *Smoking/No Smoking* and *Private Fears in Public Places*, which relied on a homogeneous type of transition [...] here the transitions are not systematic. They are forgotten during the last quarter of the first act [only] to [...] reappear just before the end of the act in the form of a mole which [...] sticks out its muzzle while looking, astonished [...]. This mole [...] will be the film's mascot. (Thomas, 2016)

While the above highlights how *Life of Riley* featured less than a fifth of the number of shots contained in *Muriel*, which might lead one to conclude that Resnais had scaled things back over the course of fifty-

Alain Resnais on the set of *Life of Riley*.

plus years, the meticulousness of Resnais' approach had in no way diminished, and François Thomas' use of the phrase "all out" tells us as much. The presence of the mole also demonstrates how Resnais, after *Je t'aime, je t'aime* and *My American Uncle*, wasn't quite done with his mischievous rodent friends.

People sometimes question how hands-on older, veteran directors are when it comes to their films, and it is frequently implied that such filmmakers delegate their duties to an extent that far exceeds what was typical in their younger days, yet it is clear that the nonagenarian Resnais was just as involved with *Life of Riley* as he was with *Hiroshima mon amour* at the very start of his feature film career. Alain Resnais was one filmmaker who had no interest in simply putting his name to a project; if anything, it seems the reverse is true, as his on-screen credit was often buried amidst those of his colleagues. For all the effort Resnais put into the scripts for his films, he never took a writing credit (*Mélo* and *Not on the Lips* have no named screenwriter, although Resnais was certainly the one who adapted both pieces) until his final three films—even then, he adopted the pseudonym "Alex Reval". It is clear that Resnais worked hard on *Life of Riley*'s screenplay, and always looked to effect the smallest of changes if they would tighten up the film:

> Resnais estimates the result at one hour and fifty-four minutes (excluding credits), then, in the company of Herbiet, he reduces the scenario by eight minutes, continuing in the logic of previous cuts with mainly small, scattered tightening, without affecting the number of shots. The work is all the easier as the two men had left certain passages "suspended" in order to give themselves time to reflect before sorting them out. The new version incorporating these changes is dated 4 September [2012]. After this date, the alterations will be done without Herbiet or [screenwriter Jean-Marie] Besset. They will mainly concern additional cuts and the overhaul of transitions. (ibid.)

As already mentioned, *Life of Riley* unsurprisingly plays as something of a composite of *Smoking/No Smoking* and *Private Fears in Public Places*, and its aesthetic lies somewhere between the full-bore artifice of the former and the airier, slightly more naturalistic look of the latter, despite *Life of Riley* being another entirely studio-bound affair. At times, the film veers into altogether uncharted visual territory for Resnais, as the actors perform in front of a hand-drawn cross-hatch backdrop when it's time for their close-ups. While *Life of Riley* was Alain Resnais' final film, it was his first to be shot digitally, a move necessitated by the stricter budget enforced by the commercial failure of *You Ain't Seen Nothin' Yet*. The film is a lot of fun in the same way that Resnais' previous Alan Ayckbourn adaptations are, and à la *Smoking/No Smoking* we are again treated to the highly dissonant spectacle of French-speaking characters quaffing English beer and reading British newspapers in a mock-up of a quintessentially English location, which inverts *Providence*'s setup in which an overwhelmingly English-sounding cast both drive on the right and neck a brand of whisky mainly drunk in continental Europe.

Despite having a lower budget than its predecessor, the posthumous *Life of Riley* did roughly twice the box-office business of *You Ain't Seen Nothin' Yet*. Some of the footfall may well have been due to Alain Resnais' death, but irrespective of the reasons *Life of Riley* was a much better note for Resnais to go out on than *You Ain't Seen Nothin' Yet*. As with several other films we have looked at in this book, *Life of Riley*'s release was informed by a death, only this time it was the very recent passing of its director that cast a pall on proceedings, and the situation was quite similar to the one in which *Eyes Wide Shut* (1999) entered cinemas while under the heavy shadow of the death of Stanley Kubrick. Anyone who saw *Life of Riley* on its initial theatrical run—and after missing out on *You Ain't Seen Nothin' Yet*, I made a special point of getting along to see Resnais' swansong—will remember how Alain Resnais' absence from the world, like that of George Riley in the film, was keenly felt. I drove to one of my favorite French cinemas, which is close to where *Muriel* was filmed, for the bittersweet experience of watching *Life of Riley*. I had the whole auditorium to myself for a de facto private screening of Alain Resnais' final film; one last intimate exchange in a public place.

Looking back on Alain Resnais' career in features, it is easy to be reductive and conclude that the man who started out crafting intricate, arcane studies of time and memory wound up filming adaptations of creaky British farces. Resnais' post-*Love Unto Death* films all look deceptively slight, but each one of these films is a deep, detailed work whose cheerful, even frivolous air belies its importance. Alain Resnais clearly had no wish to attempt to sustain the intensity of *Hiroshima mon amour*, *Last Year at Marienbad*, *Muriel* and *Je t'aime, je t'aime*, if indeed such a move was even possible. It would have been easy for Resnais to have ceased making feature films after *Je t'aime, je t'aime*, in much the same way that Elem Klimov lost interest after his shattering masterpiece *Come and See* (*Idi i smotri*, 1985), feeling that he'd achieved everything that was possible as far as cinema was concerned. Yet the same familiar concerns would manifest themselves time and again, as Resnais examined relationships, loss, regret, absence, guilt, grief, the past, and so on. Even if a film looked, or even *felt*, like a minor divertissement—*Life of Riley* being a good example—there was usually a great deal more to it.

As mentioned earlier in this book, *Muriel* stands as Alain Resnais' finest achievement, and although he would probably not want to consider that he'd peaked with the third of his twenty feature films, nothing subsequent to it ever hit quite the same heights—although *Je t'aime, je t'aime* came pretty close. To make such a claim may appear tantamount to dismissing Resnais' post-1960s output, but that is not the intention; rather, it highlights *Muriel*'s brilliance, as Resnais' filmography is littered with challenging, engaging and thought-provoking films. It just so happens that *Muriel* is the pick of what is an embarrassment of riches, and it remains the densest of stars around which Resnais' other films orbit. Part of *Muriel*'s greatness lies in the way in which it pulls together all of Resnais' major preoccupations: time, memory, historical trauma. Jim Hoberman, in addition to detecting a hint of the theatricality that would come to the forefront in Resnais' later works, summarized the way in which *Muriel* represents both the best of Resnais and the crystalizing of its director's obsessions:

> *Muriel, or The Time of Return* […] can be considered his quintessential film. As revisited in Criterion's excellent new Blu-ray transfer, […] it also appears to be his greatest. […] The screenplay supplies the exits and entrances of a stage play. But the largely associative montage is highly

cinematic and overtly modernist, based less on the characters' histrionics than a sense of clashing vectors and visual force fields. At times, Mr. Resnais intercuts multiple conversations or matches the sound of one interaction to the image of another so that the movie seems to be talking to itself. […] In essence, *Muriel* is a series of ruptures—both for Mr. Resnais's characters and within his film—that serve to dramatize the way in which war and colonialism can disrupt individual lives as well as conventional narratives. (2016)

Few other filmmakers have put together such a consistently interesting body of work, and that Alain Resnais was able to maintain such a standard over his fifty-five year career in features is little short of remarkable. They certainly broke the mold when they made Resnais, and his singularity is comparable to that of Delphine Seyrig; both of these key players in the story of *Muriel* now lie in Paris' Montparnasse Cemetery. No filmmaker before or since Alain Resnais has managed to manipulate time in quite the same way, although there is a contemporary director in Christopher Nolan who has successfully employed intricate temporal shifts and elliptical editing in films including *Memento* (2000), *Inception* (2010), *Interstellar* (2014), *Dunkirk* (2017) and *Tenet* (2020); like Resnais, Nolan has frequently, unfairly been accused of being a cold, clinical filmmaker. In recent years, arguably the best example of a film that explores time in the fluid manner so typical of Resnais has come in the form of Bertrand Bonello's magnificent, spellbinding *House of Tolerance/House of Pleasures* (*L'Apollonide: Souvenirs de la maison close*, 2011). Outside of *Je t'aime, je t'aime*, Resnais' ability to bend time didn't involve science fiction, and he always seemed far more interested in the individual's perception, as opposed to the universal concept, of time.

Throughout this book I have attempted to convey just what makes *Muriel, or The Time of Return* so special. A flick back through the previous pages will confirm that consideration of *Muriel* ultimately takes us, just like its characters, sprawling off into a number of directions and areas: memory, the Algerian War, the OAS, behaviorism, the French New Wave, lost love, colonialism, Boulogne-sur-Mer, André Malraux, torture, the Second World War, time (and time travel), Delphine Seyrig, theater, Alain Resnais' wider filmography, and so on. The discussion on *Muriel* involving Jacques Rivette et al., which was referenced way back in the introduction, reinforces how a film about, inter alia, absence leads us to examine so many things that occur outside of the frame. *Muriel* is so highly condensed that opening it up leads to a great deal of unpacking, and it is a film that eagerly invites us to read around what it presents. While I firmly believe that *Muriel* works as a discrete film—as any wholly successful movie should—it also prompts us to delve into so many diverse subjects and concepts. *Muriel* sends us into some dark territory we may not be keen to traverse, and the descriptions of the tortures of Henri Alleg and Djamila Boupacha make for grim reading, as do the accounts of the bombing of little Delphine Renard's home and the premature deaths of André Malraux's two sons and their mother. Yet there is a sense that knowledge of everything surrounding, and therefore contributing to, *Muriel* is worthwhile.

Muriel's Françoise (Nita Klein).

I used to think that *Muriel*'s barely-begun love affair between Hélène and Alphonse seemed an impossibly inconsequential slice of melodrama, one that should not be sharing a space with the very real issues of torture and the Algerian War—in much the same way that I felt (and still feel) that James Cameron's *Titanic* (1997) places more importance on a fictional romance than a maritime disaster in which more than 1500 people lost their lives. On subsequent viewings of *Muriel*, however, I began to see the film through the eyes of Resnais and Jean Cayrol: the tale of Hélène and Alphonse isn't at the center of *Muriel*—the story of Bernard and Muriel forms the black heart of the film—but it is largely up to the viewer to separate the important from the trivial.

In *Muriel*, Alain Resnais presents us with many different things in an even, measured manner, with no real clues as to what should take priority, or which events carry more meaning. It doesn't take many viewings to see that the game played by Hélène and Alphonse—and I'm still not completely sure as to what those two are up to—is of little relevance to anyone but them, although both parties clearly see it as a more pressing business than the damaged Bernard and/or the war he participated in. Ernest, who admittedly may have a dog in this fight, appears to share my outlook on Hélène and Alphonse, given that he

The sign for Boulogne's Rue de Folkestone, a street which symbolizes the pasts of both the town and Hélène, features prominently in *Muriel*.

Out with the old: Nausicaá, the aquarium that stands on the former site of *Muriel*'s casino, September 2017.

growls, "We never knew what you two wanted" as the wheels well and truly fall off the Sunday lunch at Hélène's. Yet without the framing soap opera of Hélène and Alphonse's incipient relationship, we wouldn't be able to gauge the gravity of Bernard's terrible secret—although we might come to wish we hadn't delved into his troubled mind.

Upon seeing Robert Bresson's astonishing *Au hasard Balthazar* (1966), which starred his future wife Anne Wiazemsky, Jean-Luc

Godard declared that "this film is really the world in an hour and a half". I would dare to propose that Alain Resnais' *Muriel*, which its director once described as "a story for everyone", similarly has it all—the sublime and the ridiculous, the workaday and the magical, the sacred and the profane—and it tells us more about ourselves than we would ever want to know.

Bibliography

Alleg, Henri, *La Question*, Paris: Les Éditions de Minuit, 1958.

Baldoli, Claudia and Knapp, Andrew, *Forgotten Blitzes: France and Italy under Allied Air Attack, 1940–1945*, London: Continuum, 2012.

Benayoun, Robert, '*En attendant Harry Dickson*: Entretien avec Alain Resnais' in Goudet, Stéphane (ed.), *Positif, revue de cinéma: Alain Resnais*, Paris: Éditions Gallimard, 2002.

——, '*Muriel, ou les rendez-vous manqués*' in ——, *Positif, revue de cinéma: Alain Resnais*, Paris: Éditions Gallimard, 2002.

Bergan, Ronald. 'Michael Lonsdale obituary.' *The Guardian*. Guardian Media Group, 22 Sept. 2020. Web. 29 Sept. 2020. <https://www.theguardian.com/film/2020/sep/22/michael-lonsdale-obituary>.

Bounoure, Gaston, *Alain Resnais, Cinéma d'aujourd'hui* 5, Paris: Éditions Seghers, 1962.

Brangé, Mireille, *Delphine Seyrig: Une vie*, Paris: Nouveau Monde éditions, 2018.

Brody, Richard, *Everything Is Cinema: The Working Life of Jean-Luc Godard*, New York: Holt, 2008.

———, 'Notes on *Cahiers*.' *The New Yorker*. Condé Nast, 11 Sept. 2010. Web. 25 Sept. 2020. <https://www.newyorker.com/culture/richard-brody/notes-on-cahiers>.

Buache, Freddy, *Le cinéma français des années 60*, Renens: Éditions 5 Continents, 1987.

Canby, Vincent. "Jeanne Dielman,' Belgian.' *The New York Times* 23 Mar. 1983: 25. Print.

Carroll, Lewis, *The Hunting of the Snark*, London: Macmillan, 1876.

Carswell, Richard, *The Fall of France in the Second World War*, Cham: Palgrave Macmillan, 2019.

Cayrol, Jean, *Muriel*, Paris: Éditions du Seuil, 1963.

Chick, Kristine Robbyn. *Re-framing French culture: Transformation and renewal in the films of Jean-Luc Godard, Alain Resnais, Agnès Varda and Jacques Tati (1954–1968)*. 2011. University of Glasgow, PhD thesis. <http://theses.gla.ac.uk/3101/>.

Croombs, Matthew. 'Algeria Deferred: The Logic of Trauma in *Muriel* and *Caché*.' *Scope*. University of Nottingham, Feb. 2010. Web. 4 Mar. 2020. <http://www.nottingham.ac.uk/scope/documents/2010/february-2010/croombs.pdf>.

De Baecque, Antoine and Toubiana, Serge, *Truffaut: A Biography* (Catherine Temerson, Trans.), Toronto: Random House, 1999.

De Beauvoir, Simone. 'Pour Djamila Boupacha'. *Le Monde* 2 June 1960: n. pag. Print.

Eliot, T. S., *Poems: 1909–1925*, London: Faber, 1925.

Ellinger, Kat, *Devil's Advocates: Daughters of Darkness*, Liverpool: Auteur, 2020.

Empson, John. 'Edward Jenner, slayer of the "speckled monster"'. *World Health Forum* 17 (1996): 351. Print.

Evans, Martin, *Algeria: France's Undeclared War*, Oxford: Oxford University Press, 2012.

———, et al. (eds), *The Algerian War and the French Army, 1954–62: Experiences, Images, Testimonies*, Basingstoke: Palgrave Macmillan, 2002.

Forsyth, Frederick, *The Day of the Jackal*, London: Random House, 1971.

Gielgud, John, *An Actor and His Time*, London: Sidgwick and Jackson, 1979.

Hartley, L. P., *The Go-Between*, London: Hamish Hamilton, 1953.

Hillier, Jim (ed.), *Cahiers Du Cinéma: The 1960s (1960–1968): New Wave, New Cinema, Reevaluating Hollywood*, Cambridge: Harvard University Press, 1986.

Hoberman, J. 'The Power of Memories: 'Muriel' and 'Cemetery of Splendor''. *The New York Times*. The New York Times Company, 25 Aug. 2016. Web. 31 July 2020. <https://www.nytimes.com/2016/08/28/movies/the-power-of-memories-muriel-and-cemetery-of-splendor.html>.

Howell, Jennifer, *The Algerian War in French-Language Comics: Postcolonial Memory, History, and Subjectivity*, Lanham: Lexington Books, 2015.

Hyde, Lewis, *Alcohol and Poetry: John Berryman and the Booze Talking*, Dallas: Dallas Institute of Humanities and Culture, 1986.

Kael, Pauline, *I Lost It at the Movies*, New York: Bantam, 1965.

Kelley, Raina. 'Snap Judgment: Books.' *Newsweek*. Newsweek Digital LLC, 19 Mar. 2006. Web. 9 Nov. 2020. <https://www.newsweek.com/snap-judgment-books-106091>.

Kennedy, Caroline and Beschloss, Michael, *Jacqueline Kennedy: Historic Conversations on Life With John F. Kennedy*, New York: Hyperion, 2011.

Kerekes, David and Slater, David, *Killing for Culture: From Edison to Isis: A New History of Death on Film*, London: Headpress, 2016.

King, Stephen, *Doctor Sleep*, New York: Scribner, 2013.

Kirsch, Scott and Flint, Colin (eds), *Reconstructing Conflict: Integrating War and Post-War Geographies*, Farnham: Ashgate, 2011.

Kunz, Edward. 'Henri Laborit and the inhibition of action.' *Dialogues in Clinical Neuroscience* 16.1 (2014): 113–117. Print.

Lack, Roland-François. 'The point in time: precise chronology in early Godard.' *Studies in French Cinema* 3.2 (2003): 107. Print.

Legrand, Laurent. 'Stavisky se suicide "d'une balle tirée à 3 mètres!".' *Le Point*. Le Point Communication, 6 Feb. 2014. Web. 29 July 2020. <https://www.lepoint.fr/histoire/stavisky-se-suicide-d-une-balle-tiree-a-3-metres-06-02-2014-1788723_1615.php>.

Leutrat, Jean-Louis, *BFI Film Classics: L'Année dernière à Marienbad* (Paul Hammond, Trans.), London: British Film Institute, 2000.

—— and Liandrat-Guigues, Suzanne, *Alain Resnais: liaisons secrètes, accords vagabonds*, Paris: Cahiers du Cinéma, 2006.

Lopate, Phillip. '*Night and Fog.*' *The Criterion Collection*. N.p., 23 June 2003. Web. 6 November 2020. <https://www.criterion.com/current/posts/288-night-and-fog>.

Macfarlane, Steve. 'Review: Alain Resnais's *Je t'aime, Je t'aime.*' *Slant Magazine*. Slant Magazine LLC, 10 Feb. 2014. Web. 22 July 2020. <https://www.slantmagazine.com/film/je-taime-je-taime/>.

Madsen, Axel, *Malraux: A Biography*, New York: Open Road, 2015.

Malraux, André, *Anti-Memoirs* (Terence Kilmartin, Trans.), New York: Holt, 1968.

"Mathieu Amalric on Alain Resnais." *YouTube*, uploaded by Film at Lincoln Center, 23 Mar. 2015, <http://youtu.be/1ZAFnIy9lco>. Accessed 23 Sept. 2020.

McMahon, Laura. 'Untimely Resnais: *Muriel*'s Disarticulations of Justice.' *Film-Philosophy*. Edinburgh University Press, Oct. 2016. Web. 31 July 2020. <https://doi.org/10.3366/film.2016.0012>.

Monaco, James, *Alain Resnais*, New York: Oxford University Press, 1979.

Pollock, Griselda and Silverman, Max, *Concentrationary Imaginaries: Tracing Totalitarian Violence in Popular Culture*, London: I. B. Tauris, 2015.

Quinan, Christine. 'Postcolonial Memory and Masculinity in Algeria: Alain Resnais's Absent 'Muriel'.' *Interventions*. Routledge, Mar. 2016. Web. 12 Mar. 2020. <https://doi.org/10.1080/1369801X.2016.1142881>.

Quint, Peter E. 'Hiroshima Mon Amour.' *The Harvard Crimson*. The Harvard Crimson, Inc., 27 Sept. 1960. Web. 18 Aug. 2020. <https://www.thecrimson.com/article/1960/9/27/hiroshima-mon-amour-pihiroshima-mon-amouri/>.

Renard, Delphine, *Tu choisiras la vie*, Paris: Éditions Grasset, 2013.

Robson, Leo. 'The Film That Yields Nothing on a Second Viewing—or a First.' *The New Yorker*. Condé Nast, 3 Jan. 2017. Web. 25 Sept. 2020. <https://www.newyorker.com/culture/culture-desk/the-film-that-yields-nothing-on-a-second-viewing-or-a-first>.

Rosenbaum, Jonathan. '*Je t'aime, je t'aime* (1973 review).' *Jonathan Rosenbaum*. N.p., 21 Feb. 2020. Web. 17 July 2020. <https://www.jonathanrosenbaum.net/2020/02/je-taime-je-taime-1973-review-2/>.

———, 'Trapped in Time: Alain Resnais' *Je t'aime, je t'aime*.' *Jonathan Rosenbaum*. N.p., 22 Apr. 2018. Web. 23 July 2020. <http://www.jonathanrosenbaum.net/2018/04/trapped-in-time-alain-resnais-je-taime-je-taime/>.

Semprún, Jorge, *La guerre est finie*, Paris: Éditions Gallimard, 1966.

Shakespeare, William, *The Tragedy of Julius Caesar*, Oxford: Clarendon Press, 1911.

Sharpe, Mani. 'Questioning female subjectivity in Alain Resnais's *Muriel*.' *Graduate Journal of Social Science* 9.3 (2012): 98–100. Print.

Shepard, Todd, *The Invention of Decolonization: The Algerian War and the Remaking of France*, Ithaca: Cornell University Press, 2006.

Sontag, Susan. '*Muriel, ou le temps d'un retour*.' *Film Quarterly* 17.2 (1964): 24–27. Print.

Sparks, Benjamin J. *The War Without a Name: The Use of Propaganda in the Decolonization War of Algeria*. 2011. Brigham Young University, MA thesis. <https://scholarsarchive.byu.edu/etd/2921>.

Thomas, François, *Alain Resnais, les coulisses de la création: entretiens avec ses proches collaborateurs*, Paris: Armand Colin, 2016.

Tintillier, Daniel, *Boulogne-sur-Mer*, Lille: La Voix du Nord, 1997.

Truffaut, François, *The Films in My Life* (Leonard Mayhew, Trans.), New York: Simon & Schuster, 1985.

Vaughan, Hunter, *Where Film Meets Philosophy: Godard, Resnais, and Experiments in Cinematic Thinking*, New York: Columbia University Press, 2013.

Vincendeau, Ginette, *Stars and Stardom in French Cinema*, London: Continuum, 2000.

Wallace, David Foster, *Infinite Jest*, New York: Little, Brown, 1996.

———, *The Pale King*, New York: Little, Brown, 2011.

Interview With New Wave Editor Ken Rowles

Appendix A

KEN ROWLES IS A FILMMAKER who has enjoyed a career spanning more than six decades. In addition to editing Jean-Luc Godard's *Sympathy for the Devil/One Plus One* (1968), he has produced a number of feature films including *Venom/The Legend of Spider Forest* (1971) and *The Ups and Downs of a Handyman* (1976). His directorial efforts include *Go Girl* (1972), *The Perils of Mandy* (1980) and *Take an Easy Ride* (1976); the last of these originated as a public information film before morphing into an exploitation movie, one which played for 48 consecutive weeks in London's West End en route to becoming a firm cult favorite.

Rowles continues to develop projects, and in recent times he has directed a documentary on the SS Richard Montgomery, a WWII Liberty ship that, despite being loaded with unexploded ordnance, still sits at its wreck site less than thirty miles from London. Just a few years ago, he made a rare appearance in front of the camera as one of the interview subjects in *Respectable: The Mary Millington Story* (2016).

* * *

Darren Arnold: *With regard to* Muriel's *editing, the film contains around 1000 shots, and during the film's first sequence there are more than 20 cuts in just 30 seconds. Alain Resnais, like you, trained and worked as an editor before directing his own films, and I think that his editor's eye was always evident in the films he made—particularly* Muriel. *Have* *you found that your editor's instinct is always there with the films you produce and/or direct, but don't actually edit?*

Ken Rowles: That's a lot of shots, as although it obviously depends on the length of the film, you're probably looking at around 400–500 shots in a typical film, so *Muriel* has roughly double what you'd expect. But yes, once you've been an editor and then go on to make films in a different capacity, you do think of the cutting. I think you instinctively know when something's wrong with it, especially with the pace of a film. I look back on cutting commercials as playing a key role in understanding the timing in editing.

D. A.: *Prior to* Sympathy for the Devil, *Jean-Luc Godard once said he considered Alain Resnais to be the greatest editor since Eisenstein, which I think reflects very nicely on you—he clearly wasn't going to let just anyone edit his films. Over the course of 60 years, Godard has dazzled us with some intricately edited works, including his most recent film* The Image Book *(Le Livre d'image, 2018). How did* Sympathy for the Devil *end up on your editing desk?*

K. R.: The ACT [Association of Cinematograph Technicians], the union, said the film had to have a British editor, so that helped put me in the frame for the job. I was with the Film Producers Guild at that point, and over the course of several years I had edited a number of documentary films for various directors, including David Cobham. Anyway, I had just edited a film for producer Eleni Collard [Eleni Cubitt] called *The Inn Way Out* (1967). Eleni was the one who was setting up *Sympathy for the Devil*, and she asked me if I would edit it.

D. A.: *Godard was clearly looking to shake it up with this film, in several ways. It was his 17th film—actually his 16th when he started it, but he made* A Film Like Any Other *(Un film comme les autres, 1968) halfway through. In the previous year, Godard had made* Two or Three Things I Know About Her… *(Deux ou trois choses que je sais d'elle…, 1967) with* Muriel's *producer Anatole Dauman; like most of Godard's New Wave films,* Two or Three Things *had been shot by his regular cinematographer Raoul Coutard, yet he chose the young Tony Richmond* *to photograph* Sympathy for the Devil. *Richmond went on to work on several Nicolas Roeg films, and he was only in his mid-20s at the time of* Sympathy for the Devil, *while you were of a similar age. Godard was approaching 40 at that point, and there's a sense that he wanted younger collaborators for the film, possibly because of the political waves people roughly your age were making in France at the time.*

K. R.: I think it was more Eleni Collard who put the team together. I think she had more to do with it than Godard. Thanks to that [film], the man who financed it, Michael Pearson, gave me my first picture [*Venom*] to produce.

D. A.: *I think it's interesting that Godard, who has often been called the filmmaker of the 1960s, made a film featuring a band—The Rolling Stones—many considered to be the band of that decade. Godard had agreed to make the film providing that either The Beatles or the Stones would be in it, which says much about his status at that time. Apparently Paul McCartney wanted to do it, while John Lennon was keen to meet Godard but refused to be filmed in the studio—although he obviously changed his mind on that as* Let It Be *(1970) was filmed the following year. Of course, Godard had come to prominence before either band, but I think no-one was ready for the way in which 1968 saw him tear up the rule book. It was the year when he formed the Dziga Vertov Group and pretty much abandoned narrative film, and* Sympathy for the Devil *demonstrates how radical his methods had become; it was a long way from pop star vehicles like* A Hard Day's Night *(1964). He'd said that* Sympathy for the Devil, *which marked his English-language debut, was to be his last "bourgeois" film, but it seems he abandoned that ambition and started his radical period a bit earlier than planned.*

K. R.: Yes, I think it was quite a shock to everyone! Having the Stones involved was just an excuse for the financing, really, so I think that [the Stones' presence] was what Pearson was interested in. What shocked the office, and Pearson himself, more than anything, was that we would arrive on a Monday morning—this was after the Stones material had been shot—only to find that the police had arrested somebody for spraying swastikas on the side of a Rolls Royce in [London's] Park

Lane, and Pearson had to pay up! He [Godard] just went out with Tony Richmond and did this stuff, no permission or licenses or anything. I remember going out to Battersea for the scrapyard scenes, and seeing it all happening.

As far as The Beatles were concerned, Lennon's life obviously changed a lot after he got together with Yoko Ono. Yoko and her previous husband, [Anthony] Cox, actually came to my cutting room to edit a film they were working on.

D. A.: *Bringing it back to Alain Resnais and* Muriel: *in the same year as* Sympathy for the Devil, *Resnais released* Je t'aime, je t'aime, *which I think is second only to* Muriel *as far as Resnais' achievements are concerned.* Je t'aime, je t'aime *showcased his editing skills in a very different way, seeing as it contained roughly one-third of the number of shots featured in* Muriel, *which brought it more in line with a typical film. With* Je t'aime, je t'aime, *it seemed as if Resnais was perfecting the themes of time and memory he'd been working on all along, whereas at the very same time Godard was actively dismantling his own approach. Godard said that the lengths of the takes for* Sympathy for the Devil *would be largely determined by the lengths of film supplied by Kodak, and he had a special magazine fitted to allow for extra-long loads of film. Yet the editing process was obviously a lot more complicated, as you were frequently moving between the documentary footage of the Stones at work and the avant-garde agitprop sequences featuring Anne Wiazemsky, et al.*

K. R.: You know that Godard took the film back to France and did his own cut? He had another editor work on it, then it came back to me to do another recut, which became the *Sympathy for the Devil* we have now. From the point of getting the film back from France, it was mainly a case of me working on it with [producer] Iain Quarrier.

D. A.: *In* Muriel, *it could be said that there's two films in there: one a routine, almost soap opera-like tale of a woman meeting up with an old flame, the other a dark investigation into the very real issue of torture in the Algerian War—a conflict Godard had examined in* Le petit soldat. Sympathy for the Devil *could also be said to be two films in one,*

Appendix A: Interview with New Wave Editor Ken Rowles

Jean-Luc Godard in 1968.

especially as the two distinct elements of the film were shot either side of another film. Plus, by the end of filming, the director seemed more interested in the Black Panthers than the Rolling Stones, a band whose involvement had obviously played a huge part in getting the film greenlit. I'd imagine pulling it all together was quite tricky for an editor. I mean, how did you get it all on the same page? What were the instructions?

K. R.: It's tricky, especially when you don't have a script (*laughs*). To be honest, the storyboard was the answer, as that was basically the guide to piecing it all together. But this is where Godard took control—we did the first assembly, then he took over. I think there were two different ideas, and it was all being pulled together by Eleni Collard. Because, when she originally came to me, she said she was making a film with The Beatles, and I think that was really what she wanted, and then she brought Pearson into it on that basis, and he was greatly attracted to it—I mean, he funded it completely. Now, as I said, there wasn't really a script as such, but rather it was a case of what was in Godard's head. The studio shoot at Barnes [Olympic Studios] was very much a case of, well, let it roll, and you can see that in the way that it was just filming the Stones doing their session. You know they set fire to the roof?

D. A.: *Yes—there was a problem with one of the lights?*

K. R.: That's right. And that became my biggest problem, as I had to sort out all the insurance stuff! Not the insurance for the film, but rather the insurance for the actual studios, because of the damage caused. The insurance company was coming in to see me so they could look at the rushes to see how the fire started. I worked very closely with the production manager, and let's just say that the two of us were controlling the problems (*laughs*). It's probably where I picked up some of my producer skills. Michael must have thought something of it, as he then offered me the chance to join him.

D. A.: *So, you finished editing the film, and the producers weren't completely happy with what Godard had come up with, so some changes were requested. Were you surprised to discover you'd have to edit a second, slightly more commercial version of the film?*

K. R.: Well, the first cut had a much more rebellious nature to it, which wasn't good for Pearson, as he was a friend of the [British] royal family!

D. A.: *One thing that stands out in the editing in* Sympathy for the Devil *is the way in which the song evolves, and we witness it progressing from an early sketch to something that takes a very recognizable shape at around the film's halfway mark. It's priceless footage of the Stones at work, although it's really just the Mick Jagger and Keith Richards show, in many ways, but it underlines how focused and driven those two were, which I think will surprise many. Richards even plays bass on the track, with Bill Wyman's contributions mainly limited to playing some percussion. And of course, there are some lingering shots of Brian Jones, who would be dead within a year of these recording sessions concluding.*

K. R.: Yes, they never started work until about 11 p.m., which is when they'd arrive at Barnes to do it, and they just worked through the night. They were serious about the work, and you really get that feeling from the film. Jagger certainly knew what he was doing, and that's still the case today.

D. A.: *And audiences didn't know which version of the film they'd be watching, as cinemas tended to interchange the two titles—*

K. R.: The French version—say, if you went and bought a copy of One Plus One in Paris—which version would you be getting?

D. A.: *Well, because directors in France always get final cut—it's the law, basically—the disc includes both versions, but I think the producers cut is probably included, or at least looked upon, as a bonus feature.*

In Muriel, *the sound editing is interesting—at times, the sound of one interaction matches the image of another, and in* Sympathy for the Devil *there's an element of this: at the start, it seems like the Stones footage and the narrative portion are two discrete elements, yet dialogue that's clearly from the fictional material is eventually heard over the work in the recording studio. And of course, the finished version of the title song plays over that magnificent closing shot of Wiazemsky on the camera crane. There's also the much-commented-on sight of Brian Jones—who for one reason and another had become a peripheral figure in the band by this stage—strumming on a guitar we can't hear. This technique creeps in quite organically, I think.*

K. R.: In fact, if you look at older movies, they cut on the cut, as it were, and nowadays sound is—well, if you look at, say [UK television serial] *Eastenders* (1985–), you get the upcoming sound before you cut to the next [scene]. I think it's just a way to make the edit run smoothly—sound is bringing you into the next scene. A lot of it's really just down to storytelling: your picture is telling one story while your sound is telling another. As I said earlier, I think editing commercials tends to be good training for this—anyone who's cut commercials tends to be a better editor than someone who's only cut drama, feature films and so on. Working on commercials teaches a certain style of editing. So with *Muriel*, the sound is telling you another story to the one you're seeing; in these moments, it's building a story using sound instead of pictures. And there are obviously cases where a different editor works on the sound, and you start with an assembly edit, then sound can be re-recorded—and the dubbing editor is usually a different person.

But I think the Brian Jones thing was to do with the film's soundtrack, and not what was actually happening in the recording studio. And, as you say, there's that moment when the final mix of the song is heard at the very end during the scene on the beach, which is the sort of thing Quarrier wanted more of—probably more than Pearson did.

D. A.: *At that point in his career,* Sympathy for the Devil *was Godard's most expensive film, and I'm guessing the producers were expecting a big and immediate return from their investment. When they heard that Godard had ideas to film it on 16 mm, almost like an amateur film, they told him he had no choice but to shoot on 35 mm, and it's clear that they had a much more commercial endeavor in mind. Yet the premiere at the 1968 London Film Festival has gone down in history all for the wrong reasons: before being ejected from the venue, Godard punched one of the producers [Quarrier] and told the audience to demand refunds. Were you there for that screening?*

K. R.: Yes, I was up in the projection box for that! The two versions thing was really the source of all the trouble.

D. A.: *Godard first arrived in London at the end of May 1968, a month which has gone down in history in France because of the civil unrest which virtually brought the country to a standstill. It's been said that Godard was reluctant to leave France at this time—back in the 60s, it seems he was wary of his status as a non-French national and was concerned he might have visa problems, although in this case I think it was probably more because he didn't want to miss out on what he hoped would be a revolution. The world was a much bigger place back then, but did you have a sense of what had been developing just a few miles across the [English] Channel?*

K. R.: Yes, well, you had the Paris riots, which is where Godard had come from, and we were due to start filming—I can remember the day—and he didn't turn up. I was probably more aware of the situation in France than the [British] man in the street was, mainly because I was working on a Godard film, but really there was only the odd [UK] newspaper article on the subject.

D. A.: *A couple of years ago, the film was treated to a 4K restoration for its 50th anniversary. Obviously, the film isn't going anywhere, but do you think that audiences are still unsure of what the film really is? I mean, there are other reference points for British bands in 60s movies, including: The Beatles' roles in* A Hard Day's Night *and* Help! *(1965); The Yardbirds appearing in Antonioni's* Blow-Up *(1966); and The Zombies in* Bunny Lake is Missing *(1965). Each of these films possesses a very clear sense of the band's place, but in* Sympathy for the Devil *that's not really the case, as the Stones aren't explicitly linked to the narrative. Mick Jagger would make Donald Cammell and Nic Roeg's* Performance *(1970) in the same year, which probably also confuses the issue.*

K. R.: I think if the film had been totally about the Stones, just a documentary on them, it would be looked on quite differently. But because it had—at least in their eyes, I'd have thought—all this rubbish, I mean, I don't think it helped them sell the record because it [the film] was, you know, shelved for ages. New Line picked it up for America, and it was mainly shown on the campus circuit. In general, the Stones didn't really want the public to see how they worked and recorded, so the footage really is something special.

I could take the film today and make it just a Stones documentary, a 30-minute film that just included the footage of them at work in the studio recording *Sympathy for the Devil*. In the studio footage, there actually isn't much editing, as most of it is made up of tracking shots, plus a few shots of the sound crew. There were a lot of films during that period that included long tracking shots like that.

D. A.: *I suspect someone's already produced a Stones-only edit and it's somewhere out there on the internet!*

Sympathy for the Devil *was produced by Cupid Productions, a company you'd go on to join, and just a few years later you and Michael Pearson would produce* Venom *at around the same time Cupid did* Vanishing Point *(1971). Also, Françoise Pascal, who appeared in*

Sympathy for the Devil *and is perhaps best known for the sitcom* Mind Your Language *(1977–1986), would turn up in your pilot for* Go Girl, *so there are a couple of connections here with your later work.*

K. R.: Françoise was friends with Simon Brent, who starred in Venom, so that's how we got her to do *Go Girl*. She's actually working on something with a friend of mine right now. She's not the same Françoise these days—we're all a bit different now (*laughs*). As for Michael, it was quite funny to think that I was working with one of the richest men in Europe.

D. A.: *Finally, I wanted to ask you about a project of yours I can't find very much on—the BFI [British Film Institute] has an entry for a film called* Torment, *which you're credited as directing. The late Rutger Hauer is the only cast member listed, while the screenwriter is given as Christian Bel, who wrote and produced the Lauren Bacall–Anthony Quinn film* A Star for Two *(1991), which is Bel's only credit on the IMDb [Internet Movie Database].* A Star for Two's *story bears some superficial similarities to the basic plot of* Muriel: *a couple reunites many years after a wartime romance, plus one of the main characters is called Alphonse.*

K. R.: Yes, well, it [*Torment*] was one that never got made, and it only got as far as pre-production. I was going to Paris every few weeks to meet up with Christian, and then he got the Bacall–Quinn film, and the film we were doing together, *Torment*, just didn't get made. This was around 1989. I was going to be the director of it, and we were going to film a lot of it in Paris, but some of it was going to be shot in Tunisia, so we went over there to look at locations. Christian spent a lot of money setting it up. *Torment* was about the Algerian War, and the main character was living in what was then present-day Paris, but in his mind he was experiencing the torment of returning to the conflict in Algeria.

D. A.: *And so* Torment *brings us back to* Muriel.

Alain Resnais Filmography

Appendix B

Hiroshima mon amour. France/Japan, 1959, 91 minutes. Screenwriter: Marguerite Duras. Producer: Anatole Dauman. Cinematography: Sacha Vierny, Michio Takahashi. Editors: Henri Colpi, Jasmine Chasney, Anne Sarraute. Music: Georges Delerue, Giovanni Fusco. With Emmanuelle Riva, Eiji Okada, Stella Dassas, Bernard Fresson.

Last Year at Marienbad (*L'Année dernière à Marienbad*). France/Italy, 1961, 94 minutes. Screenwriter: Alain Robbe-Grillet. Producer: Anatole Dauman. Cinematography: Sacha Vierny. Editors: Henri Colpi, Jasmine Chasney. Music: Francis Seyrig. Assistant Director: Florence Malraux. With Delphine Seyrig, Giorgio Albertazzi, Sacha Pitoëff, Françoise Bertin.

Muriel, ou le temps d'un retour (*Muriel, or The Time of Return*). France/Italy, 1963, 116 minutes. Screenwriter: Jean Cayrol. Producer: Anatole Dauman. Cinematography: Sacha Vierny. Editors: Kenout Peltier, Eric Pluet. Music: Hans Werner Henze. Stills Photographer: Liliane de Kermadec. Assistant Director: Florence Malraux. With Delphine Seyrig, Jean-Pierre Kérien, Jean-Baptiste Thiérrée, Nita Klein, Jean Champion, Jean Dasté, Françoise Bertin, Martine Vatel.

The War Is Over (*La Guerre est finie*). France/Sweden, 1966, 122 minutes. Screenwriter: Jorge Semprún. Producer: Anatole Dauman. Cinematography: Sacha Vierny. Editors: Ziva Postec, Eric Pluet. Music: Giovanni Fusco. Assistant Director: Florence Malraux. With Yves

Montand, Ingrid Thulin, Geneviève Bujold, Michel Piccoli, Jean Dasté, Anouk Ferjac, Martine Vatel, Françoise Bertin, Jean-Pierre Kérien.

Je t'aime, je t'aime. France, 1968, 94 minutes. Screenwriter: Jacques Sternberg. Producer: Mag Bodard. Cinematography: Jean Boffety. Editors: Colette Leloup, Albert Jurgenson. Music: Krzysztof Penderecki. Assistant Director: Florence Malraux. With Claude Rich, Olga Georges-Picot, Anouk Ferjac, Bernard Fresson.

Stavisky.... France/Italy, 1974, 117 minutes. Screenwriter: Jorge Semprún. Producer: Jean-Paul Belmondo. Cinematography: Sacha Vierny. Editor: Albert Jurgenson. Music: Stephen Sondheim. Assistant Director: Florence Malraux. With Jean-Paul Belmondo, Michael Lonsdale, François Périer, Anny Duperey, Claude Rich, Charles Boyer, Gérard Depardieu.

Providence. France/Switzerland, 1977, 107 minutes. Screenwriter: David Mercer. Producer: Yves Gasser. Cinematography: Ricardo Aronovich. Editor: Albert Jurgenson. Music: Miklós Rózsa. Assistant Director: Florence Malraux. With John Gielgud, Ellen Burstyn, Dirk Bogarde, David Warner, Elaine Stritch, Denis Lawson.

My American Uncle (*Mon oncle d'Amérique*). France, 1980, 126 minutes. Screenwriter: Jean Gruault. Producer: Philippe Dussart. Cinematography: Sacha Vierny. Editor: Albert Jurgenson. Music: Arié Dzierlatka. Assistant Director: Florence Malraux. With Gérard Depardieu, Nicole Garcia, Henri Laborit, Pierre Arditi, Roger Pierre.

Life Is a Bed of Roses (*La Vie est un roman*). France, 1983, 111 minutes. Screenwriter: Jean Gruault. Producer: Philippe Dussart. Cinematography: Bruno Nuytten. Editor: Albert Jurgenson. Music: Philippe-Gérard. Assistant Director: Florence Malraux. With Fanny Ardant, Vittorio Gassman, Geraldine Chaplin, Ruggero Raimondi, Sabine Azéma, André Dussollier, Marie Rivière.

Love Unto Death (*L'Amour à mort*). France, 1984, 93 minutes. Screenwriter: Jean Gruault. Producer: Philippe Dussart.

Cinematography: Sacha Vierny. Editors: Albert Jurgenson, Jean-Pierre Besnard. Music: Hans Werner Henze. Assistant Director: Florence Malraux. With Pierre Arditi, Fanny Ardant, Sabine Azéma, André Dussollier, Jean Champion, Jean Dasté.

Mélo. France, 1986, 110 minutes. Screenwriter: Alain Resnais (uncredited). Producer: Marin Karmitz. Cinematography: Charles Van Damme. Editor: Albert Jurgenson. Music: Philippe-Gérard. Assistant Director: Florence Malraux. With Fanny Ardant, Sabine Azéma, Pierre Arditi, André Dussollier, Catherine Arditi.

I Want to Go Home. France, 1989, 105 minutes. Screenwriter: Jules Feiffer. Producer: Marin Karmitz. Cinematography: Charles Van Damme. Editor: Albert Jurgenson. Music: John Kander. Executive Mentor: Florence Malraux. With Adolph Green, Gérard Depardieu, Laura Benson, Linda Lavin, Caroline Silhol, Jean Champion, Françoise Bertin, John Ashton, Micheline Presle.

Smoking/No Smoking. France/Italy/Switzerland, 1993, 140/145 minutes. Screenwriters: Jean-Pierre Bacri, Agnès Jaoui. Producer: Michel Seydoux. Cinematography: Renato Berta. Editor: Albert Jurgenson. Music: John Pattison. With Sabine Azéma, Pierre Arditi.

Same Old Song (*On connaît la chanson*). France/UK/Italy/Switzerland, 1997, 122 minutes. Screenwriters: Agnès Jaoui, Jean-Pierre Bacri. Producer: Bruno Pésery. Cinematography: Renato Berta. Editor: Hervé de Luze. Music: Bruno Fontaine, Henri Christiné. With Agnès Jaoui, André Dussollier, Pierre Arditi, Sabine Azéma, Jean-Pierre Bacri, Lambert Wilson, Jane Birkin, Jean-Pierre Darroussin, Françoise Bertin.

Not on the Lips (*Pas sur la bouche*). France/Switzerland, 2003, 117 minutes. Screenwriter: Alain Resnais (uncredited). Producer: Bruno Pésery. Cinematography: Renato Berta. Editor: Hervé de Luze. Music: Maurice Yvain, Bruno Fontaine. With Isabelle Nanty, Audrey Tautou, Lambert Wilson, Sabine Azéma, Pierre Arditi, Jalil Lespert, Darry Cowl.

Private Fears in Public Places (*Cœurs*). France/Italy, 2006, 125 minutes. Screenwriter: Jean-Michel Ribes. Producer: Bruno Pésery. Cinematography: Éric Gautier. Editor: Hervé de Luze. Music: Mark Snow. With Isabelle Carré, Sabine Azéma, Pierre Arditi, Laura Morante, André Dussollier, Lambert Wilson, Claude Rich.

Wild Grass (*Les Herbes folles*). France/Italy, 2009, 104 minutes. Screenwriters: Alain Resnais (as Alex Reval), Laurent Herbiet. Producer: Jean-Louis Livi. Cinematography: Éric Gautier. Editor: Hervé de Luze. Music: Mark Snow. With André Dussollier, Emmanuelle Devos, Sabine Azéma, Mathieu Amalric, Anne Consigny, Roger Pierre, Sara Forestier, Michel Vuillermoz.

You Ain't Seen Nothin' Yet (*Vous n'avez encore rien vu*). France, 2012, 115 minutes. Screenwriters: Alain Resnais (as Alex Reval), Laurent Herbiet. Producer: Jean-Louis Livi. Cinematography: Éric Gautier. Editor: Hervé de Luze. Music: Mark Snow. With Mathieu Amalric, Anne Consigny, Lambert Wilson, Sabine Azéma, Pierre Arditi, Michel Piccoli, Anny Duperey, Denis Podalydès, Michel Vuillermoz, Vimala Pons.

Life of Riley (*Aimer, boire et chanter*). France, 2014, 108 minutes. Screenwriters: Alain Resnais (as Alex Reval), Laurent Herbiet, Jean-Marie Besset. Producer: Jean-Louis Livi. Cinematography: Dominique Bouilleret. Editor: Hervé de Luze. Music: Mark Snow. With Sandrine Kiberlain, Sabine Azéma, Caroline Silhol, André Dussollier, Michel Vuillermoz, Hippolyte Girardot.

Photo Credits

Appendix C

† Image dates from the theatrical/home video release of the film and was issued to press outlets for publicity purposes.

‡ Denotes a Creative Commons license as accepted by Wikimedia Commons. Details on the various CC licenses can be found at: http://creativecommons.org/licenses.

Introduction:

"*Muriel*'s Alphonse (Jean-Pierre Kérien) and Hélène (Delphine Seyrig)". Photo courtesy of Eureka Entertainment.†

"The main entrance to the *Muriel* building, February 2020". Photo by the author.

"The lonely sign on the wall of the *Muriel* building, February 2020". Photo by the author.

Chapter 1:

"François Truffaut in Amsterdam, 1965". Photo by Jack de Nijs/Anefo, uploaded under the description "Franse regisseur Francois Truffaut voor bioscoop Cinétol, waar zijn film draait [Le Peau Douce?] tijdens Nouvelle Vague festival, 15 maart 1965". CC0.‡

"The sign for the street where much of *Muriel* unfolds, October 2019". Photo by the author.

"An aerial view of Boulogne-sur-Mer". Uploaded by Daniel P, under the description "Boulogne vue aérienne de la cathédrale". Public Domain.

Chapter 2:

"A catch of tuna fish being unloaded in Boulogne". Uploaded by Daniel P, under the description "Boulogne débarquement du thon". Public Domain.

"Calais, May 1940". Courtesy of Bundesarchiv, Bild 101I-383-0337-11/ Böcker. Modified from the original (cropped). CC BY–SA 3.0.‡

"Boulogne's war memorial". Photo by Lep62 (Chris), uploaded under the description "Monument aux morts de Boulogne-sur-Mer". CC BY–SA.‡

"The *Muriel* building, February 2020". Photo by the author.

"The plaque on the *Muriel* building, February 2020". Photo by the author.

"*Muriel*'s "pretty hideous" casino, which was demolished in 1987". Uploaded by Daniel P, under the description "Boulogne le casino". Public Domain.

"Boulogne's Boulevard Gambetta, pre-WWII. Note the Folkestone Hotel on the left". Scanned and uploaded by Claude Villetaneuse, under the description "Carte postale ancienne éditée par LL, n°29: Boulogne-sur-Mer—Le Quai Gambetta". Modified from the original (cropped). Public domain.

"Boulogne-Tintelleries station, February 2020". Photo by the author.

Chapter 3:

"Henri Alleg in 2008". Photo by (:Julien:), uploaded under the description "Henri Alleg at the Fête de l'Humanité 2008". Modified from the original (cropped). CC BY–SA 4.0.‡

"*Muriel*'s Hélène (Delphine Seyrig) investigates Bernard's workroom". Photo courtesy of Eureka Entertainment.†

"Djamila Boupacha in 2017". Photo by Brahim Djelloul Mustapha, uploaded under the description "Madame Djamila Boupacha, grande Moudjahida durant la guerre d'Algérie". CC BY–SA 4.0.‡

"Plaque commemorating the Paris massacre of 1961". Photo by Claude Shoshany, derivative work Lämpel, uploaded under the description "Plaque commémorative du massacre des algériens lors de la manifestation du 17 octobre 1961 sous les ordres du Préfet de Police Maurice Papon, implantée sur la Passerelle de la Fraternité à Aubervilliers". Modified from the original (cropped). CC BY–SA 3.0.‡

"Caroline Huppert in 2018". Photo by JohnPDeauv, uploaded under the description "Caroline Huppert 2018". CC BY–SA 4.0.‡

Chapter 4:

"Delphine Seyrig in 1969". Photo by Wonder6789, uploaded under the description "Delphine Seyrig as Laïs in Fernando Arrabal's *The Garden of Delights* (Paris, 1969)". CC BY–SA 4.0.‡

"Delphine Seyrig as Hélène in *Muriel*". Photo courtesy of Eureka Entertainment.†

Chapter 5:

"André Malraux in 1974". Photo by Roger Pic, uploaded under the description "André Malraux". Public domain.

"Alain Delon in 1959". Photo by Licio D'aloisio/Reporters Associati & Archivi /Mondadori, uploaded under the description "L'acteur français Alain Delon à la table d'un café sur la Via Veneto à Rome, le 5 octobre 1959". Public domain.

Chapter 6:

"Jorge Semprún in 2009". Photo by Dinkley, uploaded under the description "Jorge Semprun, à La Comédie du livre de Montpellier, 23 mai 2009". CC BY–SA 3.0.‡

"The poster for *Je t'aime, je t'aime*'s 2015 home video release". Photo courtesy of Kino Lorber.†

"Olga Georges-Picot (right) in Alain Robbe-Grillet's *Successive Slidings of Pleasure*". Photo courtesy of Kino Lorber.†

Chapter 7:

"Sandrine Kiberlain and André Dussollier in *Life of Riley*". Photo courtesy of Eureka Entertainment.†

"The poster for the 2018 re-release of *My American Uncle*". Photo courtesy of Potemkine.†

"Sandrine Kiberlain in *Life of Riley*". Photo courtesy of Eureka Entertainment.†

"Alain Resnais (far right) on set with the cast of *You Ain't Seen Nothin' Yet*". Photo courtesy of Kino Lorber.†

"Alain Resnais on the set of *Life of Riley*". Photo courtesy of Eureka Entertainment.[†]

"*Muriel*'s Françoise (Nita Klein)". Photo courtesy of ORTF.[†]

"The sign for Boulogne's Rue de Folkestone, a street which symbolizes the pasts of both the town and Hélène, features prominently in *Muriel*". Photo by the author.

"Out with the old: Nausicaá, the aquarium that stands on the former site of *Muriel*'s casino, September 2017". Photo by the author.

Appendix A:

"Jean-Luc Godard in 1968". Photo by Gary Stevens, uploaded under the description "Jean-Luc Godard at Berkeley, 1968". CC BY 2.0.[‡]

www.ingramcontent.com/pod-product-compliance
Lightning Source LLC
Chambersburg PA
CBHW051059160426
43193CB00010B/1245